ROY HART AND THE EARLY ROY HART THEATRE

Roy Hart's revolutionary work on the human voice through extended vocal technique and the Wolfsohn-Hart tradition has influenced several generations of practitioners. Hart's outstanding contribution to vocal research, practice and performance stretched over 20 years until his untimely death in 1975, and his vocal training produced performers with extraordinary and highly expressive vocal ranges. He founded a theatre company, Roy Hart Theatre, that brought his ideas to realisation in groundbreaking works. His influence, through his own use of the voice for theatre and music and its embodiment in his company, was widespread, attracting the interest of directors such as Peter Brook, Jerzy Grotowski and Jean-Louis Barrault.

This book combines:

- a detailed biography giving the social and artistic context of Hart's work and that of the early Roy Hart Theatre
- an exploration of Hart's own writings on his work, combined with a review of articles by his wife Dorothy Hart and in-depth interviews
- a stylistic analysis of his key works, including *The Bacchae, and, L'Economiste* and *Biodrame*, and their critical reception
- pathways into some of the practical exercises devised by close collaborators of Roy Hart and practitioners of the Roy Hart Theatre Tradition.

As a first step towards critical understanding, and as an initial exploration before going on to further, primary research, *Routledge Performance Practitioners* offer unbeatable value for today's student.

Kevin Crawford was a founding member of the Roy Hart Theatre and much of this book is informed by his memories of his performing life with the company, and his professional work afterwards as a theatre and voice practitioner working in France, Italy, Ireland, England and elsewhere.

Bernadette Sweeney has a PhD in theatre from Trinity College Dublin and is Professor of Theatre and Performance Studies and head of Acting at the University of Montana School of Theatre and Dance. She is lucky to have been able to train with Kevin in various workshops in Ireland and France over a period of years, and also with other Roy Hart and Pantheatre company members.

ROUTLEDGE PERFORMANCE PRACTITIONERS

Series editors: Franc Chamberlain and Bernadette Sweeney

'Small, neat (handbag sized!) volumes; a good mix of theory and practice, written in a refreshingly straightforward and informative style… *Routledge Performance Practitioners* are good value, easy to carry around, and contain all the key information on each practitioner - a perfect choice for the student who wants to get a grip on the big names in performance from the past hundred years.' - *Total Theatre*

Routledge Performance Practitioners is an innovative series of introductory handbooks on key figures in contemporary performance practice.

Each volume focuses on a theatre-maker who has transformed the way we understand theatre and performance. The books are carefully structured to enable the reader to gain a good grasp of the fundamental elements underpinning each practitioner's work. They provide an inspiring springboard for students on twentieth century, contemporary theatre, and theatre history courses.

Now revised and reissued, these compact, well-illustrated and clearly written books unravel the contribution of modern theatre's most charismatic innovators, through:

- personal biography
- explanation of key writings
- description of significant productions
- reproduction of practical exercises.

Volumes currently available in this series:

Joan Littlewood by Nadine Holdsworth
Jacques Copeau by Mark Evans
Jacques Lecoq by Simon Murray
Mary Wigman by Mary Anne Santos Newhall
Hijikata Tatsumi and Ohno Kazuo by Sondra Fraleigh and Tamah Nakamura
Bertolt Brecht by Meg Mumford

Ariane Mnouchkine by Judith G. Miller
Vsevolod Meyerhold by Jonathan Pitches
Jerzy Grotowski by James Slowiak and Jairo Cuesta
Augusto Boal by Frances Babbage
Konstantin Stanislavsky by Bella Merlin
Pina Bausch by Royd Climenhaga
Anna Halprin by Libby Worth and Helen Poynor
Eugenio Barba by Jane Turner
Rudolf Laban by Karen K. Bradley
Tadeusz Kantor by Noel Witts
Michael Chekhov by Franc Chamberlain
Marina Abramovic by Mary Richards
Robert Wilson by Maria Shevtsova
Etienne Decroux by Thomas Leabhart
Robert Lepage by Aleksandar Saša Dundjerovic
Frantic Assembly by Mark Evans & Mark Smith
Jana Sanskriti by Ralph Yarrow
Antonin Artaud by Blake Morris
Roy Hart by Kevin Crawford and Bernadette Sweeney

For more information about this series, please visit: https://www.routledge.com/Routledge-Performance-Practitioners/book-series/RPP

ROY HART AND THE EARLY ROY HART THEATRE

Kevin Crawford and Bernadette Sweeney

LONDON AND NEW YORK

Cover credit: Illustration (c) Ben Piggott

First published 2022
by Routledge
2 Park Square, Milton Park, Abingdon, Oxon OX14 4RN

and by Routledge
52 Vanderbilt Avenue, New York, NY 10017

Routledge is an imprint of the Taylor & Francis Group, an informa business

© 2022 Kevin Crawford and Bernadette Sweeney

The right of Kevin Crawford and Bernadette Sweeney to be identified as authors of this work has been asserted by them in accordance with sections 77 and 78 of the Copyright, Designs and Patents Act 1988.

All rights reserved. No part of this book may be reprinted or reproduced or utilised in any form or by any electronic, mechanical, or other means, now known or hereafter invented, including photocopying and recording, or in any information storage or retrieval system, without permission in writing from the publishers.

Trademark notice: Product or corporate names may be trademarks or registered trademarks, and are used only for identification and explanation without intent to infringe.

British Library Cataloguing-in-Publication Data
A catalogue record for this book is available from the British Library

Library of Congress Cataloging-in-Publication Data
A catalog record for this book has been requested

ISBN: 978-0-367-21833-1 (hbk)
ISBN: 978-0-367-21834-8 (pbk)
ISBN: 978-0-429-26643-0 (ebk)

DOI: 10.4324/9780429266430

Typeset in Perpetua
by Apex CoVantage, LLC

CONTENTS

List of figures   ix
List of abbreviations   xi
Acknowledgements   xiii

1 BIOGRAPHY AND INFLUENCES   1

     Introduction 1
     Early years 4
     The Wolfsohn years 6
     The Ridgeway years (1962–7) 11
     Roy Hart's career as a vocal soloist 16
     The Abraxas Club: The birth of Roy Hart theatre (1967–74) 31
     L'Economiste and Malérargues (1974–5) 37
     Who was Roy Hart? 41

**2 ROY HART AND DOROTHY HART:
WRITINGS, INTERVIEWS, LETTERS**   43

     Introduction 43
     Writings 44
     The interviews 55
     The writings of Dorothy Hart 59
     Roy Hart's letters 67
     Conversations and private letters 70

3   FOUR PRODUCTIONS BY RHT (1967–76)   75

The Bacchae 75
and 88
Biodrame 95
L'Economiste 102

4   PATHWAYS TO THE HUMAN VOICE: IN THE FOOTSTEPS OF ROY HART AND ROY HART THEATRE   115

Paradoxes and pathways 115
Waking up the voice 118
Breath, bone, muscle, sound 120
Kevin Crawford's Malérargues Workshop – Summer 2019 138
Exploring Height and Depth: The Lift by Noah Pikes 145
Passing The Sound by David Goldsworthy 148
Three Letters, Three Times, Three Minutes
   by Pascale Ben 151
Touch – Be in Touch – Be Touched: Through Touch
   into Voice Towards Music by Edda Heeg 155

Bibliography   **161**
Index   **169**

FIGURES

1.1	Roy Hart and Kevin Crawford, image courtesy of Ivan Midderigh, RHT Photographic Archives.	3
1.2	Roy Hart and Karlheinz Stockhausen, image courtesy of Ivan Midderigh, RHT Photographic Archives.	27
1.3	Roy Hart with Roy Hart Company performing *Kyrie Eleison*, St. Pancras Church London, image courtesy of Ivan Midderigh, RHT Photographic Archives.	30
2.1	Personal letter from Roy Hart to the Roy Hart Company (RHT Archive), image courtesy of Ivan Midderigh, RHT Photographic Archives.	71
3.1	Dorothy Hart with the chorus of *The Bacchae* 1969, image courtesy of Ivan Midderigh, RHT Photographic Archives.	76
3.2	The chorus of *and* in performance 1972, image courtesy of Ivan Midderigh, RHT Photographic Archives.	88
3.3	*L'Economiste* 1975, image courtesy of Ivan Midderigh, RHT Photographic Archives.	103
4.1	Exercise 4.3: The Pelvic Clock with actor Aimee Paxton, image by Bernadette Sweeney.	121

4.2 Exercise 4.4: Sacra-Lumbar Stretch, with actor
Aimee Paxton, image by Bernadette Sweeney. 123

4.3 Exercise 4.4: Sacra-Lumbar Stretch: Variation 1,
with actor Aimee Paxton, image by Bernadette Sweeney. 124

4.4 Exercise 4.5: Standing Variations of The Pelvic Clock,
with actor Aimee Paxton, image by Bernadette Sweeney. 127

4.5 Exercise 4.11: Waking Up Centres of Resonance with a
Short Text, with actor Aimee Paxton, image by
Bernadette Sweeney. 140

ABBREVIATIONS

RHT   Roy Hart Theatre

CAIRH   *Centre Artistique International Roy Hart* (Roy Hart International Artistic Centre)

PA   *Primer Acto*

ORTF   *Office de Radiodiffusion Télévision Française* (former National French Radio and Television Network 1964–74)

ACKNOWLEDGEMENTS

We are very grateful for the input of so many company members in the development and publication of this work – any errors are ours alone. We honour the work of Roy Hart and all company members, and offer our heartfelt thanks to the many Roy Hart Theatre Company members who shared their memories and artistry with us for this project, including Noah Pikes, Richard Armstrong, Kaya Anderson, Linda Wise, Paul Silber, Nadine George, Ian Magilton, Enrique Pardo, Jonathan Hart, Margaret Pikes and Saule Ryan.

In Chapter Four company members and/or Hart practitioners share elements of their studio practice with us – we thank Noah Pikes, David Goldsworthy, Pascale Ben, Edda Heeg and Richard Armstrong for bringing their skills and vision and entering into this collaborative space with us and eventually into the studios of every reader of this work. For the photographic materials included here we thank RHT member and photography archivist Ivan Midderigh and University of Montana MFA graduate actor Aimee Paxton.

Unless otherwise stated, all translations are either existing translations from the RHT Archives without clear authorship or they are by Kevin Crawford. Thanks to Stefan Koch for his assistance in reviewing translations from German.

Acknowledgements

Our sincerest thanks to *Routledge Performance Practitioners* Series Editor Franc Chamberlain and also at Routledge to Zoë Forbes and Ben Piggott for their patience and guidance throughout this project.

We thank the Roy Hart Centre and the *SCI de Malérargues* for generously offering a research residency to Kevin Crawford and for allowing Bernadette Sweeney and Kevin Crawford full access to the RHT Archives. In this respect we acknowledge the essential role Clara and Paul Silber have played in organising and maintaining these archives until their retirement. Likewise, Ivan Midderigh's Roy Hart Theatre Photographic Archives are a precious resource and record of the company's history. We thank Carol Mendelsohn and Davide Maffeo for their practical assistance and Jonathan Hart who as, President of the Roy Hart Centre during the research for this book, lent us his full support. We gratefully acknowledge the support of the Office of the Dean of the College of the Arts and Media, and the Office for Research and Sponsored Programs at the University of Montana.

We would also like to acknowledge the work and commitment of the many actors that have participated in training workshops with us, especially those in Kevin's summer workshop in Malérargues July 2019 and Bernadette's MFA and BFA acting studios at the University of Montana 2020–1, persevering throughout the pandemic. We encourage any reader/practitioner who is interested in pursuing this work more fully to contact the *Centre Artistique International Roy Hart* in Malérargues, France to investigate fuller opportunities in training and research: https://roy-hart-theatre.com/

Bernadette Sweeney is grateful for the ongoing support of colleagues at the University of Montana School of Theatre and Dance throughout this project, most especially Erin McDaniel, John DeBoer, Jason McDaniel, Heidi Eggert and Dr. Pamyla Stiehl, as we worked together to figure out how to continue to research, perform and work in studio and online throughout the recent pandemic.

Finally, as always, our love and thanks to our families:

KC: For Caroline, Clelia, Natacha and Sara and my guiding parents Christina and Monty.

BS: For Bryan, Ruby and Saoirse, for my parents and siblings and in memory of Tony, who is still leading the way.

1

BIOGRAPHY AND INFLUENCES

INTRODUCTION

Roy Hart made an outstanding contribution to vocal research, practice and performance over a twenty-year period from the middle of the twentieth century until his untimely death in 1975. As a soloist, he lent his prodigious vocal skills to twentieth-century composers who were redesigning the limits of voice in contemporary music theatre. He founded a theatre company, Roy Hart Theatre, that brought his ideas to realisation in groundbreaking works, which attracted immense interest both in the United Kingdom and throughout Europe and South America. His influence, through both his own use of the voice for theatre and music and its embodiment in his company, was widespread, as attested by the interest of leading lights of the day, such as directors Peter Brook, Jerzy Grotowski and Jean-Louis Barrault. In many ways, he was at the forefront of a (not so quiet!) revolution of how we regard voice work today, and how we redefine the relationship between voice as an expression of the person, and voice as it manifests itself in performance. His story is a powerful reflection of a period in recent history where a small nucleus of artists dedicated themselves to challenging views that limited exploration of the voice's boundaries and hidden potential, and, in so doing, questioned accepted conventions in making and presenting theatre.

We have called this book *Roy Hart and The Early Roy Hart Theatre* because, although it is centred around the founding company figure of Roy Hart, the company's work was actually more collaborative than a focused study of him as the central figure would imply. Therefore, we look here at the evolution of the company, and focus on its work under the leadership of Hart, until shortly after his death. We recognise that the work of the company continued beyond that point, but that later phase, as the company consolidated its roots in French and international theatre, is not considered closely here. We are lucky to be able to reference the work of many company members through our study of archive materials and our documentation of the history of the company from its early beginnings in London through its relocation to France and its compelling and inventive productions throughout Europe in the 1970s and beyond. We look to the life of Roy Hart as our starting point and he remains a central figure throughout the work of the company and our chapters here. However, as you will see, much of our evidence is drawn from the writings of those around Hart and those who continue the work into the twenty-first century. Also, the work of the company lives on in the embodied practices of company members like author Kevin Crawford, Jonathan Hart, Linda Wise, Noah Pikes, Kaya Anderson and the many others who have gone on to found companies, publish books and become leaders in the field of voice training for theatre and performance. For example, Enrique Pardo, Linda Wise and the late Liza Mayer established Pantheatre of Paris which continues to disseminate and expand on Hart practices. Noah Pikes went on to write one of seminal texts on Hart, *Dark Voices*, and contributes exercises to **Chapter Four** of this book. Jonathan Hart and Richard Armstrong have both made a lasting contribution to the Experimental Theatre Wing at New York University and continued to amplify the scope of vocal performance in contemporary music theatre. Nadine George, through her Voice Studio International, trains teachers in her approach to voice, and Margaret Pikes in collaboration with Patrick Campbell has recently authored *Owning Our Own Voices, Vocal Discovery in the Wolfsohn-Hart Tradition* (Routledge, 2020). These are just some examples of the global reach of the original company members and subsequent associate artists, and their influence on international voice practice and pedagogy. As mentioned, this book mirrors this shared heritage as we include contributions and exercises from four other company members and/or Hart practice teachers in **Chapter Four** of this book: Noah Pikes, David Goldsworthy, Edda Heeg and Pascale Ben.

Chapter One of this book looks at the early years of Hart and the forming of the company through to its rich production phase up to Hart's decease in 1975 and the dissemination of the work through the many and varied careers of the company members as voice teachers and practitioners.

In **Chapter Two** we look to detail the principles of Hart and company members through the traces of practice we found in production documents, interviews and letters. Hart did not leave behind a fully documented theory of his practice, but those who embodied the practices in their work with him and after his death have provided many insights into the work that help to detail the methodology in studio training and in performance.

In **Chapter Three** we look to a number of productions including: *The Bacchae*, *Biodrame* and *L'Economiste* to give evidence of the work in performance, and to give the reader insights into how this sometimes esoteric work translated into production. This chapter is enhanced by the testimonies of performance as detailed by Kevin Crawford and other company members.

Figure 1.1 Roy Hart and Kevin Crawford, image courtesy of Ivan Midderigh, RHT Photographic Archives.

Finally, in **Chapter Four** we look to offer you, the reader, a set of workshop principles through the listed exercises, so as to give you an embodied route into the work. Much of the work was advanced and developed by a fully dedicated company, but the principles are fundamental and hopefully accessible to you in this way. We are grateful for the contributions of some other company members here, as listed in the chapter, and feel that this sharing of workshop practices is an appropriate reflection of the continuing life of the work through its many members, and their students who form a new generation of Hart practitioners.

EARLY YEARS

Roy Hart was born Reuben Hartstein to Polish-Lithuanian parents in Johannesburg, South Africa on 30 October 1926. After an Orthodox Jewish education, he studied English, history of music, philosophy and psychology at Witwatersrand University, Johannesburg. Already at school his talent for theatre and in particular his vocal talents had been noticed and at university he took on major roles in theatre productions, culminating in playing the leading role in *Peer Gynt* by Ibsen in 1946. Derek Rossignol, who was, by a twist of fate, to later become a founder member of his company, Roy Hart Theatre, recalls having seen him perform: '(his) performance of Peer Gynt was most impressive – you'd have thought he was already professional!' (Pikes 2019: 79). Shortly after this he decided to leave South Africa, and travel to England where he became the recipient of a coveted scholarship to the Royal Academy of Dramatic Art (RADA).

In May of 1947 he commenced his studies at RADA, London, this time using the name Royden Hart. The acting teacher at that time wrote in his first report from summer 1947: 'Has talent but is in need of intensive technical training to make full use of it. A good voice and great vitality and force, when he will make use of them. His main difficulty is his re-action to criticism' (RADA 1947). A later report that same year refers again to his 'talent and great "weight" on the stage, unusual in a student' (RADA 1947) but reiterates that he must learn to accept criticism.

On 5 June 1947, quite early on in his studies at RADA, Roy Hart met **Alfred Wolfsohn**. He recounted how he first met him in an interview with José Monleón: 'The family who I lived with told me that since I had such a good voice why shouldn't I see a good friend of theirs who dealt with the voice? It was Wolfsohn' (Monleón, Estruch and Domenech 1971). This first meeting with Wolfsohn had a profound impact on Hart and he immediately wrote about it in his diary, describing Wolfsohn as 'a man who I feel has the ability to bring out the very best in me. ... He is indubitably the finest thing that has happened in my life. He has I feel evidently "seen" or felt in me something deep and meaningful not just another otiose artist' (Roy Hart unpublished diary 1947).

> **Alfred Wolfsohn** (1896–1962) was a charismatic and highly unconventional voice teacher, who, as a German Jew, had fled Nazi Germany and settled in London in 1939. His experiences as a soldier during the First World War had left him profoundly traumatised. In particular, he was haunted by the screams of wounded, anguished soldiers that he had heard on the battlefield. In order to heal his wounded spirit, he found that music and in particular singing brought solace, and reaffirmed his search for meaning in a world that seemed to have gone mad in war. His ideas, expressed in his book *Orpheus or The Way to a Mask* and in his unpublished manuscripts, propose a radical revisioning of how we approach the voice. He believed that the voice was a profound mirror of the soul, and that the development of the voice was a key to personal individuation. Vocal problems and difficulties had a psychological origin and he needed to address these in his pupils in order to heal their voices. He had the gift of deep complicity with his students and was instrumental in guiding them to intense self-discovery through his voice classes. Wolfsohn is now recognised as being a visionary figure who forged a profound reappraisal of the potential of the human voice (Wolfsohn 2012).

Hart's engagement with Wolfsohn created some conflict and tension with his studies at RADA, but he did complete the two-year span of study. Hart felt that he was torn between the text-based work on the voice as practiced at RADA and Wolfsohn's approach which seemed to emphasise the sound over the word. In addition he was profoundly influenced by the personal and philosophical implications of Wolfsohn's work which contrasted with the more limited vision of the actor as he perceived it at RADA. Above all he was preoccupied with his deep need to find authenticity and vocal embodiment as an actor. His attempts to explain what he was doing with Wolfsohn were met with derision by his fellow students and his teachers remarked on what they called 'over-voicing' which was surely a side-effect of Wolfsohn's work on range extension. Clifford Turner, who was to have a lasting influence on voice teaching in the UK through his book *Voice and Speech in the Theatre* (1950), wrote in his last report on Hart: 'A good voice here, but he is inclined to over-voice although there has been a marked improvement in this' (RADA 1949).

By the spring of 1949, at the end of his second year, Hart was still getting good reports. The school's principal wrote: 'He has a robust sense of dramatic expression. He has imagination which he must use more precisely to present characters, not himself. He deserved his free fee exhibition' (RADA 1949). However, he clearly disappointed his acting teacher: 'This student has the making of a good actor, but he must listen more to direction, and less to outside influence' (ibid.). Clearly this 'outside influence' refers to Wolfsohn, who was occupying an increasingly central place in Hart's training and his attitude towards theatre. This came to a head when Hart finally rejected a major role so he could continue studying with Wolfsohn. At this point both RADA and Hart's family thought he was lost. Roy Hart, however viewed his change in direction differently. He had felt for some time that there was a conflict in himself between his rabbinical origins, symbolised in his grandfather, who disapproved of theatre, and his own desire to go onstage.

Roy Hart himself described his problems as an actor in this way: 'Yet I had known for some time that my voice was not *rooted*, not literally *embodied*; that the varied roles I was considered to perform so well were actually only figments of my imagination with no connection with my body' (Roy Hart 1967). Wolfsohn offered Hart a way forward to embody or root his voice so he might perform in a more holistic fashion. To this end, Hart's studies with Wolfsohn, and this is where they also departed from the conventional training offered at RADA, included an in-depth self-examination, a testing of his own psychology and self-belief.

THE WOLFSOHN YEARS

Hart studied intensively with Wolfsohn from 1947 till Wolfsohn's death in 1962. During this time he was challenged and tested by Wolfsohn who brought formidable psychological and philosophical insight to his work, insisting on the connection between the psyche and the voice, between art and humanity. Hart has not left us a written record of these years, but its influence could be found in his evolving practice, and in the people he subsequently chose to form the theatre company with. Thoroughly immersing himself in Wolfsohn's multidimensional approach to the voice, which was much influenced by Jungian analytical psychology, was profoundly nurturing for Roy Hart. Gradually he rediscovered what he called his own embodied voice and began to repair the cleavage in himself between his deep passion for theatre and his need for moral and spiritual anchorage. His shyness gave way to renewed confidence in himself. His teaching too reinforced his conviction that this work was his life's work, as Wolfsohn would say, his 'vocation'. A key moment in Hart's studies with Wolfsohn was when he was grappling with the role of Othello in the scene of Desdemona's murder that he was due to perform (notwithstanding the concerns of playing a Black character as written by a white playwright). The breakthrough occurred when he discovered his own violence and, most importantly, the sound expressing it. Hart recalled: 'I no longer needed any decor, costume or prop to give my performance a seeming of truth' (Roy Hart '*Biodrame....is somewhat the story of my life*' 1973).

Once he had completed his studies at RADA Hart was able to concentrate fully on his work with Wolfsohn, and as Wolfsohn became indisposed owing to a recurring illness, Hart gradually assumed more responsibility and took on a teaching role, which included giving lessons to Marita Günther, Kaya Anderson, Derek Rossignol and Robert Harvey (all of whom became key founder members of Roy Hart Theatre). Hart comments on this period of his life:

> At that time we had decided to dedicate ourselves to experimentation: we were going to study a play and divided it into parts from the point of view of sounds. It was then that he got sick and since I was already working with some students I had to start taking care of the rest of the people. In this way I gained much experience.
> (Monleón, Estruch and Domenech 1971)

Already by 1955 Roy Hart was regarded as one of Wolfsohn's star pupils, and he was singled out for his interpretations of T.S Eliot, despite the vocal accomplishments of his fellow students, who sang across an impressive range. In performance Hart was using his vastly increased vocal range and palette of sounds that he had developed with Wolfsohn to bring new life and vigour to performing text. He was already finding his own path to applying his new-found skills to theatre. Wolfsohn's natural orientation in working with the voice had been a musical one, and, before the Second World War, he had mainly worked with opera singers in Berlin. It was only when he started to teach again in London in 1943 that he began the shift to working with extreme ranges of sound, breaking the accepted barriers of what was considered to be a male or female range, encouraging his students to reach out far beyond the customary bounds of singing. Hart became the closest collaborator of Wolfsohn in this most exploratory and pioneering phase. And Hart was the collaborator who could guide this work towards its theatrical possibilities, both as a soloist and as a coach to his students.

> **T.S. Eliot** (1888–1965) is recognised as being a leading figure in modern poetry, and was awarded the Nobel Prize in Literature in 1948, 'for his outstanding, pioneer contribution to present-day poetry' (The Nobel Prize n.d.). His work captured the innermost conflicts and preoccupations of twentieth-century man in poetry that was original and broke with a convention that had lost its force. *The Rock* was written as an ecclesiastical pageant (1934) and expresses Eliot's yearning for a religious awakening to contrast his despair in the face of what he viewed as modern man's loss of God.

By 1958 Roy Hart was sharing a flat with Marita Günther and Kaya Anderson, upstairs from an ailing Wolfsohn in 133 North End Road in Golder's Green, London and Hart had taken on some of Wolfsohn's teaching responsibilities. Hart had lived through the most groundbreaking years of Wolfsohn's work as a pioneer, testing the very edges of vocal possibilities and finding their corollary in the psyche and their potential application in music and performance. A whole host of sounds, not usually found in formal Western vocal expression, were called up: high flute-like whistles, cavernous roars, chorded sounds, double-stopping effects, cracked sounds, animal and machine noises. At the same time, Hart and his fellow students were able to climb seemingly effortlessly up the scale and sing confidently over four or even five octaves.

In the 1960s Hart was allowed to bring his experimental work with the voice to some of the patients at Shenley Psychiatric Hospital. Shenley had a long-standing policy of non-conventional treatments of patients including therapies such as malaria and electro-convulsive therapies and insulin injections (some of which would be considered controversial or even unethical now) and prided itself at being at the cutting edge of research.

During this time Roy Hart continued to challenge himself by applying his vocal skills and dramatic sensibility to a range of texts and authors: Rudyard Kipling, medieval poetry, Edgar Lee Masters, **Chris Mann**, Noel Coward and **Peter Redgrove**. But it was above all his renditions of T.S. Eliot that were to leave an indelible imprint on those who saw him perform in the small sound-proofed studio at 133 North End Road that had been specially converted for the work on the voice.

Chris Mann (1949–2018), was an Australian composer working in compositional linguistics. His German Jewish parents were pioneers in the fields of ethnomusicology and oral literature, and these childhood influences, combined with undergraduate studies in Chinese and linguistics at the University of Melbourne, strongly influenced his compositional style. Later interests in the philosophy of language and systems theory also reveal themselves in his music.

Peter Redgrove (1932–2003) was one of the more prolific writers of mid-twentieth-century English letters. A poet, novelist and playwright, Redgrove drew on his training as a scientist and science journalist to write collections of poetry marked by an attendance to the mystical roots of the natural world.

Company member Nadine George remembers seeing Roy Hart for the first time in 1962:

> Roy was performing *The Rock* by TS Eliot. I had seen the great actors, Olivier and Laughton in Stratford in 1956, but I had never seen anybody use their voice with this range and emotional depth and technique that Roy did. It really

> affected me very deeply and I knew I had to work with him but I didn't know why at that point. It was a real body-soul feeling that I have to work with this man on the human voice (George 2020).

During the years from 1957–62, Wolfsohn's health suffered several setbacks, although he still insisted on teaching whenever he had the strength. Inevitably Roy Hart and Marita Günther began to take on more responsibility, as did Kaya Anderson and Sheila Braggins, in caring for Wolfsohn. Hart soon had a circle of students who had had no direct contact with Wolfsohn although 'Wolfsohn sat in on some of those early lessons' (Pikes 2019: 83). He had already begun to invite some students to take part in evening drama sessions where Hart would investigate scenes from plays and bring them to life using the vocal potential they had developed in lessons with him.

It was probably during 1958 that Roy Hart met Dorothy Stuart Davidson [Findlay] and her baby son, Jonathan, whose father was David Kidaha Makwaia (1922–2007). David Kidaha was the paramount chief of the influential Sukuma federation of Tanzania, and played an important part in facilitating Tanzania's transition from British imperialism to independence. Dorothy was born in 1926 in Kenya and had returned to England when she was 4 for her schooling. She was a vivacious and artistically oriented child, excelling in music. Her studies took her to Cambridge University where she graduated with a degree in English. Dorothy Hart had met David Kidaha in Tanzania while she was working as a secretary for the British government in East Africa. She returned to England with her son and shortly after meeting Roy Hart began to take lessons with him. Thus started a relationship that was to endure until their deaths in 1975.

According to Kaya Anderson:

> Roy Hart's singing students numbered about 15 people at the time of Alfred Wolfshohn's death in in 1962. Already some years before Wolfsohn's death, Roy was giving singing lessons, private talks and acting classes to those students.
> (Anderson 2015)

In 1959 Roy represented Wolfsohn at the London Conference of Logopaedics and Phoniatrics (speech and language therapy); and in July 1961 he read a paper prepared with Wolfsohn for a meeting, possibly of the (London) Society for Analytical Psychology, outlining the connection between the psyche and the voice, using recordings of Wolfsohn's students to illustrate their findings. On 4 February 1962 Wolfsohn succumbed to a fatal staphylococcal chest infection, and he was cremated four days later. There followed a year of personal debate on Hart's part and discussion amongst Wolfsohn's core students as to whether he would take on the mantle of Wolfsohn's work:

> He had to decide whether or not he wanted to take on a burden that no one else was qualified to do. It was a decision that was neither easy or immediate., in fact he only reached it after more than a year of deep thought, during which time we all discussed the future ... and the only way he could do so was to make it his own. It had to become his work (Braggins 2011: 196).

THE RIDGEWAY YEARS (1962–7)

Over the next five years Roy Hart consolidated Wolfsohn's work, creating a first generation of students who were dedicated to his approach. Hart would usually invite students to work one on one, but would soon convene lessons with two or more students, and would then integrate them into the group sessions he had already commenced during Wolfsohn's lifetime. During this period Hart took on the role of mentor regarding the members of what was becoming a more and more stable group. His mentorship was primarily orientated towards the spiritual and artistic development of his students as they unravelled hidden vocal material and started to integrate their experiences on a pathway to self-discovery and artistic fulfilment. This could be a revelatory experience for the students and it often created long-term bonds between the students and Hart. However, as the commitment of his group strengthened, Hart found himself also in the role of lay therapist, caring for both personal and group dynamics. As the company evolved and throughout its tenure under Hart, personal relationships formed and dissolved fluidly, which brought immense challenges to Hart's mediation skills as individual members experienced profound changes in their personal and artistic lives. However, Hart and the company succeeded in this precarious balancing act, ploughing back their personal and relationship struggles into their research and performance work. A cornerstone of Hart's philosophy was the insistence on bringing life and art together in a concrete and tangible fashion. He achieved this in part by calling regular meetings for his group where dreams and personal issues were discussed against a background of readings and the study of influential writers and newspaper articles that could anchor the group's aims and struggles. These meetings, though, might equally well transform into a lesson that Hart led from the piano, where a dream, a phrase from a book, or an upsurge of emotion might be amplified and dramatised, the entire group taking part in an almost ritualistic act of vocal and dramatic catharsis. This built up a tight network of intimate knowledge between the members, 'private' lives often being shared in the 'public' domain of these meetings. Hart's insistence on the inclusion of personal relationships within the mindscape of the company as a whole was to reach a new intensity later when he revealed that he had himself started a second relationship within the company with Vivienne Young. This would play out to tragic effect later, when, on 18 May 1975 during a tour, as he was travelling by car with those closest to him, a car crash took the lives of Roy Hart, Dorothy Hart and Vivienne Young. Paul Silber was the sole survivor.

New students included Nadine George, Paul Silber, Elizabeth (Liza) Mayer, Robert Harvey, Barrie Irwin, Louis Frenkel, Monty Crawford and Anna Allen, all of whom became instrumental in the creation of a theatre company bearing Hart's name and some of whom constituted a body of teachers who gradually assumed his private teaching responsibilities. Other students also joined in these years, but some gradually withdrew as the company became more professional. The essence of this period was captured in the film *The Theatre of Being* in 1964: 'The film gives insight into the way Hart was combining psychotherapy, drama, music, and religion. In the film Hart hints at his aspirations to create a new type of society' (Pikes 2019: 82). Hart states:

> We believe that people tend to live on a monotonous and unconscious level. When individuals join the group, we try to overcome this in a variety of ways. One is by deep and complete breathing ... a natural rhythm based on breathing. Each individual has overcome internal deadness, and we are feeling and acting together as a group ... We know that everyone has a voice, not simply a speaking voice but a voice which is pure energy and comes from the whole body—in all other expressive fields what the individual is doing is external to himself but in this type of voice production he is going inward. Because of this it is an intensely personal experience.
>
> (Shephard 1964)

This film was made in the new studio that had been created in 41, The Ridgeway, a semi-detached house also in Golders Green, acquired by Dorothy Hart, where Hart was now living with Dorothy, her son Jonathan and several other members of the group: Kaya Anderson, Marita Günther, Derek Rossignol and Robert Harvey.

Hart's teaching in this period focused on 'embodying the sound', exploring and expanding the vocal, emotional and imaginative range of his students. Male students were expected to explore the highest reaches of their voices, seemingly touching sounds that were more associated with women; likewise female students would dive into the deepest, darkest vocal zones, bringing up sounds apparently more masculine in quality. This insistence on the 'hermaphroditic' nature of the voice (see **Chapter Two**), where conventions and assumptions about what a man or a woman should sound like were challenged, was a central tenet in Hart's work and often informed his and his company's performances. He also began to apply this work to textual and musical expression, to poems, to monologues and songs. Hart's core belief was that actors had to strip themselves of false and superficial acting habits in order to access a deeper layer of truth and authenticity. The group sessions, whether they were primarily in the form of meetings or collective improvisations through voice and body, were designed to increase sensitivity and break down barriers between the group members as people and performers. In this way, he was welding his students into a tight-knit group, highly receptive to each other on a kinaesthetic and intra-psychic level. Members presented songs and poems that were often orchestrated through group participation. Hart developed a shorthand method of communicating to the group during these sessions. He would sometimes use the piano to indicate tempo or volume. Other times he would call out 'Infinity': the group would freeze in silence where it was, however uncomfortable the position, and breathe fully as Hart might say 'Listen'. Concentration was intense and sustained for long periods of time, sometimes lasting more than six hours with hardly a break. Gradually more experienced members of the group would intuit where the improvisation might lead. However, members were constantly reminded not to assume that what had happened in a previous session was to be repeated in the next. Hart would always insist on responding to impulses in the present moment and he would often test his group so they remained open to the unexpected. Gradually small-scale collective pieces were developed under the supervision and inspiration of certain core members. Robert Harvey choreographed a choral version of Federico García Lorca's *Lament for the Death of Ignacio Sánchez Mejías* and Marita Günther adapted *The Love and Death of Cornet Christopher Rilke*, a prose poem written by Rainer Maria Rilke, for ensemble performance. The group became more adept at shifting out of a group improvisation into a solo rendition of a poem or song or would melt from a structured piece, like the two works mentioned above, to an open-ended silence that might portend a new exploration. A constant theme seemed to be the alternating choral and solo sequences, the one and the many: the sometimes intimidating presence of the chorus faced with the individual, or the chorus as a soothing, gentle force that could heal the individual.

In these ways Hart was laying the foundations for what was eventually to become a fully fledged theatre company. However, Hart had in a sense put aside his own aspirations as a performer to take on the role of teacher, mentor and lay therapist after Wolfsohn's death. He had succeeded in bringing together a group, that was practised in his mixture of voicework and psychic development, but he yearned to return to theatre, and his own performing potential. Nadine George recalls Hart confiding to her:

> after those five years it became very clear to me that he wanted to work with himself, that he wanted to develop his work as an artist. That's when, I remember, he said 'When new people start coming you will take over the teaching'. He said he would continue to take the meetings, chair the meetings on dreams and so on but wouldn't teach the voicework.
>
> (George 2020)

During these years Hart worked to inform leading artists, writers and scientists of the existence of his work and the group that had now constellated around it. Some leading figures were invited by Hart to visit the studio and observe the work; visitors included **R.D. Laing**, a psychiatrist well known for his work at the Tavistock Clinic and two luminaries from the world of theatre: **Peter Brook** and **Jerzy Grotowski**.

R.D. Laing (1927–89) was a Scottish psychiatrist who wrote extensively on mental illness. He was associated for a long period with the Tavistock Clinic in North London. He challenged norms in psychiatric medicine and proposed a new model for approaching mental illness based on social and psychological factors. In 1960 he wrote *The Divided Self* that summed up his thinking at that time. Through Arthur Janov and his book *The Primal Scream*, he was introduced to therapy based on vocal liberation: his encounter with Hart and his company in the early seventies allowed him to see how this work might have personal and artistic validity.

Peter Brook (1925–) is an internationally recognised director known for his outstanding contribution to theatre over a long and very successful career. Although he achieved much distinction early on with the Royal Shakespeare Company, he subsequently created the International Centre for Theatre Research, which has been based since 1974 at the Bouffes du Nord theatre in Paris. With a dedicated group of actors from a variety of nationalities and performance backgrounds, he created and trained a company that embarked on a series of dazzling theatrical experiments in far-flung locations. His landmark productions include *A Midsummer Night's Dream* for the RSC, *The Mahabharata* for the Avignon Festival and *The Tempest* for the Bouffes du Nord. He has written several books on his experiences notably *The Empty Space* (first published in 1968).

Jerzy Grotowski (1933–99) was a Polish theatre director whose ideas and innovative approach to making theatre have had a major influence on theatre in the twentieth century. Through painstaking years of research, he charted an alternative course for theatre, eschewing the attractions of spectacle, and favouring a total engagement of the actor with little or no props. He conceived of this form of theatre as 'Poor Theatre' and, following his success in Poland, he brought his work to critical acclaim in the UK and subsequently the US. Grotowski's career led him away from direction to expanding his research interests through the Theatre of Sources and the Centre for Experimentation and Theatre Research in Pontedera, Italy.

In general, though, Hart seemed to avoid direct contact with his contemporaries in the performing arts sphere. Whether this was because he felt he needed to maintain the hermeticity of his group, 'protecting' it from outside interference, or whether he was shy or unsure is hard to tell. However, he did invite these two theatre-makers who were at the forefront of experimental theatre in the early 1960s. Brook visited in 1966 and wrote afterwards: 'what they are doing could certainly be of interest and value both culturally and educationally to the English theatre as a whole' (Brook 1966). Brook was accompanied on one of these visits by Jerzy Grotowski. This first meeting between Hart and Grotowski was a mixed experience for Hart. Rossignol remembers that 'Grotowski ignored Roy altogether-he couldn't face him-and kept asking individual pupils about how Wolfsohn worked, implying Roy had deviated from Wolfsohn's path' (Pikes 2019: 87). Hart referred to Grotowski in an interview:

> Later he asked us, the Roy Hart Theatre, if we would be interested in appearing as background in a film he was making. I said no, because it seemed to me that his attitude towards certain vital situations was not the same as mine. As in the case of Peter Brook, years later he began to be interested again because he began to find our work important.
>
> (Monleón, Estruch and Domenech 1971)

Hart must have been disappointed and angry that Grotowski seemed to bypass him and be more interested in Wolfsohn, his predecessor. Given this bias on Grotowski's part, Hart probably would not have wanted his company to act as a background for the film.

By late 1967 the scene was now set for Hart and his group to move forward into a phase that would enable them to expand their operations and open their research work to an ever wider public, whilst also running a centre that could give work to some of its members. Two of the recently arrived members of the group were to play a central role in this new development: Louis Frenkel and Monty Crawford, both of them businessmen whose acumen was now in service to the vision of Hart and his group. Hart, though, began to see an opportunity for himself to emerge as a performer, using his prodigious range and, by this point, his mature acting skills.

ROY HART'S CAREER AS A VOCAL SOLOIST

Roy Hart had already, during his years of intense study with Wolfsohn, started to explore how to use his now extended vocal range in a musical setting. Conventional wisdom about vocal range in the post Second World War period attributed a range of one and a half octaves to the untrained voice and a limit of two and a half octaves to the trained opera singer. Sounds that were outside these ranges were considered ugly, unmusical or distorted. Very little music was written for a voice that defied the two-and-a-half-octave limit, and most voices were determined to stay within the rigid operatic definitions: tenor, bass, baritone for men and contralto, mezzo and soprano for women. Few performers would stray outside their strictly defined range. The emergence of the countertenor in the 1950s heralded a recognition that the male voice could stretch to pitches normally reserved for the female voice, but this recognition remained an exception. Even so, a countertenor singer was expected to remain within the proscribed range of his repertoire. A countertenor would not adventure into the lower ranges, at least not professionally. A few singers like Yma Sumac (1922–2008) had defied convention and made remarkable careers singing over a four-octave range, but their skills had rarely been used in music theatre compositions. The one notable exception was Cathy Berberian (1925–83) who had collaborated with a string of contemporary composers, in particular her husband Luciano Berio, and had already in 1966 put forward a radical review of accepted norms in her article 'The New Vocality in Contemporary Music'. Susan McClary writes:

> Music history owes a great deal to Berberian. Most obviously, her example inspired an explosion of performance artists and singers who specialize in extended vocal techniques. She made full use of rude sounds never before regarded as having a place within music, now fundamental to the work of Meredith Monk, Diamanda Galas, Laurie Anderson, and countless others.
>
> (McClary 2020: xxvi)

Hart, however, as early as 1956, was making recordings, alongside Wolfsohn's most accomplished pupils of the time, that went far beyond accepted norms for singers. In *Vox Humana*, recorded and published by Folkways Records, Hart demonstrated his ability to sing over a range of five octaves in a series of leaps while repeating the word 'Viola', and sung a theme from *Chanson Triste* by Tchaikovsky that uses a range that is below the normally accepted bass tessiture. Later recordings from 1964 included Hart singing *O Come all ye Faithfull* using what he called a chorded or multiphonic sound (the voice seems to emit several sounds on different pitches simultaneously, hence chorded), as well as using his vocal agility and mimicry skills for unconventional interpretation of several arias from Verdi operas. The recording that most represented his work in the late 1960s was called *The Eight Octave Voice*. Paul Silber recalls its making:

> In 1968, Barry Irwin and I worked out that the time had come to promote Roy's voice through making a recording of him. At this time, Roy was working hard on his voice in our new centre, the 'Abraxas Club', originally the 'Hampstead Squash Club'. Since the squash courts had a superb natural echo of their own, we proposed that the recording should take place there. [...] This one session became 'the 8 Octave Voice'......!
>
> (Silber 'The Eight Octave Voice' n.d.)

A second demonstration tape was made at this time, called *Soul Portrait*. Lasting 30 minutes, it was sent to a number of prominent composers in the hope that a work might be written that used his vast vocal range and timbres. Three key composers of contemporary music responded positively to Hart's voice either through hearing this tape or through direct contact: Hans **Werner Henze**, **Peter Maxwell Davies** and **Karlheinz Stockhausen**.

Hans Werner Henze (1926–2012) was a German composer who created very theatrical and often political works for opera in a variety of styles, including classic opera, chamber and comic opera, musicals and ballet. He experimented widely, creating pieces based on literary works, audio work and other hybrid forms. His politics were heavily influenced by his disgust for Nazism, as seen first-hand in the actions of his father, and his personal experience as an enforced member of the Hitler Youth. His works include *Maratona* (1957), *Elegy for Young Lovers* (1961), the politically controversial *The Raft of the Medusa* (1968) and *Essay on Pigs/ Versuch über Schweine* (composed 1968 and premiered 1969) which featured Roy Hart as lead vocalist. Other works include *Orpheus Behind the Wire* (1983), *Requiem* (1993), *Liebeslieder* (1985), *L'Upupa und der Triumph der Sohnesliebe* (2003) and *Phaedra* (2007). He lived most of his life in Italy.

Karlheinz Stockhausen (1928–2007). Like Henze, Stockhausen was born in Germany to a father who espoused Nazism. His mother was institutionalised when Stockhausen was a boy, and later killed by the Nazi regime. Stockhausen would go on to become one of the great musical visionaries of the twentieth century, experimenting with rhythm, precision and electronic sound. Some of his best-known works include *Kontra-Punkte* (1953), *Song of the Youths* (1956), *Gruppen* (written for three orchestras 1955–57), *Spiral* (1969) (which Roy Hart performed in) and the opera cycle *Donnerstag aus Licht* (composed over a 26-year period 1977–2003).

Peter Maxwell Davies (1934–2016) was a British composer and conductor, and is now acknowledged as one of the great twentieth century innovators in form. His early work was considered anti-establishment and, in some cases, unplayable, but he later became more accepted as his music became more melodic, and he was appointed as master of the Queen's Music in 2004. His works include the opera *Taverner*, first performed in 1972, *The Lighthouse* (1980), the controversial *Eight songs for a Mad King* (1969) – written for, and first performed by, Roy Hart – *The Last Island* (2009) and *Symphony no.10* (2014). He was committed to music education throughout his life and career, and his last work was the children's opera *The Hogboon* (2016) which premiered shortly after his death.

All three of these composers, relatively early on in their careers, were articulating their own musical language and style. In their own way each of them wished to challenge preconceptions about what constituted music. Meeting with Hart offered them a perfect opportunity to review the role of the human voice, and its contrast with instruments. Once the initial contact with these three composers had been made things moved swiftly. Within a year both Henze and Maxwell Davies had composed works inspired by Hart's voice and the theatrical and musical possibilities he offered. Francesca Placanica, in her essay 'Embodied Commitments: Solo Performance and the Making of New Music Theatre', refers to Roy Hart as 'One of the key personalities to stand out from the shifting congeries of activity merging music theatre and voice work' (Placanica 2019: 260).

Henze was first to complete a new work. It was to be called *Versuch über Schweine* (*Essay on Pigs*) (1968) and was composed immediately after the aborted premiere of his *The Raft of The Medusa* from 1968, a requiem for Che Guevara that had been highly controversial. *Versuch über Schweine* was based on a poem by the young Chilean writer Gastón Salvatore, and, like *The Raft of The Medusa*, was to be a revolutionary piece focused on the student uprising of 1968. It was also a protest against the assassination attempt on Rudi Dutschke, a prominent German student activist. Roy Hart and Henze had met in the autumn of 1968 when Hart was attending a conference on the human voice in Amsterdam. Hart and Henze met up in the director's office at the Royal Concert Hall, and Hart gave Henze a direct demonstration of his voice. Henze saw in this encounter an opportunity to connect his wish to stage social revolution with Hart's vision of personal liberation through the voice. Hart also offered Henze a vocal range and nuance that could enhance compositional possibilities for voice and orchestra.

Versuch über Schweine, performed by the English Chamber Orchestra with the Phillip Jones Brass Ensemble, premiered at the Queen Elizabeth Hall, London, on 14 February 1969, featuring Hart as the vocal soloist, with Henze himself conducting. The instruments used were woodwind, brass, percussion, strings, a beat organ and an electric guitar. While the piece lasts barely 20 minutes, it is a concentration of explosive vocal and instrumental energy, alternating moments of diabolic crescendo with softer, almost romantic segments, reminiscent of a Berlin cabaret. This piece is very successful in both contrasting and sometimes uniting the vocal and instrumental forces at the service of Salvatore's poem, poised between an impassioned revolutionary shout and a lucid, almost surgical analysis of what is possible in the real world. Henze uses Hart's vocal skills to great effect, alternating heightened moments of extreme sound with the combined attacks of brass and drums, guitar and clarinet. *Versuch über Schweine* was more an oratorio than a fully fledged music theatre piece, as Hart was later to experience in his collaboration with Maxwell Davies. Hart, as soloist, was planted firmly centre stage with a free range of movement. The musicians were placed in a conventional ensemble setting. However, the piece itself was by no means conventional, and it heralded Hart's appearance on the new music scene as a soloist of unusual powers:

> Mr. Hart, a Wolfsohn disciple, ranges through the octaves in *Sprechgesang* [vocal genre between speech and song] and sometimes achieved a kind of

double-stopping. Moreover, he mimed every word and phrase, mirroring his vocal line with large free gestures of the arms, twirling out a graphic representation of a word like *wiederkehrend* (recurring) while he spoke it. It was an uninhibited, confident, astonishing performance – and perhaps a little hard to take.

(Porter 1969)

Stanley Sadie, writing in *The Times* echoed Porter:

The chief cause of the enthusiasm was the narrator, Roy Hart, rather than the music. Mr. Hart 'sings' over some four octaves (from the Queen of Night's heights to Sarastro's depths) and growls and whistles even further. His language coupled with gestures, is remarkably expressive.

(Sadie 1969)

Hart speaks about Henze and the reasons for the breakdown in their collaboration in his paper 'The Objective Voice':

Hans Werner Henze heard my sounds and immediately wanted to use them for the externalisation of his own need for revolution. He wrote 'Versuch Über Schweine' originally for my voice, but shortly after Deutsche Grammophon recorded my performance of this work, I pointed out certain psychological facts to him, as a friend, and there has since been a rift in our relationship – to me, quite an expected pattern.

(Roy Hart 'The Objective Voice'1972)

In turn, Henze, in his autobiography, *Bohemian Fifths*, speaks critically about Hart's musicianship:

Roy Hart was a guru, not a musician: it was difficult with him, as he could neither sing well on the beat, nor react to musical entrances, to bring the work to fruition, and immediately afterwards, to make the recording of *Versuch Über Schweine*. What's more he had a problem with pitch. The day of the recording was the worst of his life. In the evening he was completely exhausted. Something good came out of this in the end for both of us: from then on Roy Hart looked in a less deprecatory way on professional musicians, so conventional to his eyes, and I admitted that, despite the revolutionary situation, working with professionals was more secure.

(Henze 1998: 251–2)

Versuch über Schweine was only performed once more after that London debut: in Lausanne almost three years later. The recording Hart and the English Chamber Orchestra made remains the only one available. Clearly the rift Hart referred to in his paper combined with Henze's realisation of the limitations of working with someone who was not a professional musician put a speedy conclusion to their partnership. However, Hart's second collaboration that year, with Peter Maxwell Davies, was not to suffer, at least initially, the same fate. Ironically Maxwell Davies also struck up a long friendship with Hans Werner Henze, when they met in London during the premiere of *Versuch über Schweine*. One wonders if they exchanged information on Roy Hart ...

Maxwell Davies and Hart had first met in 1968 at Hart's invitation. Maxwell Davies attended a rehearsal of *The Bacchae* at The Abraxas Club and wrote back to Hart:

> This was a disturbing and beautiful experience, that I'll never forget, and will always be grateful for. I was very genuinely and completely involved, and deeply moved. [...] I brought along, as you know, Randolph Stow, who is doing the poems for George III. He was knocked out too, and has done half of the poems. They are superb I think – the real thing. I'll send them as soon as I have the lot and we can meet to discuss how we tackle them.
>
> (Maxwell Davies 1968)

Maxwell Davies's project was to compose a piece based on the madness of King George III with a libretto by Australian-born writer Randolph Stow (1935–2010). *The Eight Songs for a Mad King* was to be a piece of music that would probe the nature of madness, using the extreme vocal textures Hart could summon up with a fiercely disjointed score as counterpoint. Stow had often been inspired by historical characters and places, and this was particularly the case with this libretto, which was suggested by a miniature mechanical organ playing eight tunes, once the property of George III. Randolph Stow had seen this organ and he had imagined the King struggling to teach his caged bullfinches to make the music which he could so rarely torture out of his flute and harpsichord. The eight scenes, so vivid and real for the King, are in his fantastic mind, as he is in fact confined to his own quarters. The flute, clarinet, violin and cello represent the bullfinches that the King was trying to teach to sing. At the climax of *Eight Songs* the vocal soloist snatches the violin from the birdcage to break it, as night descends and he reflects on evil. This outburst of violence, Maxwell Davies writes, 'is a giving-in to insanity, and the ritual murder by the King of a part of himself, after which, at the beginning of No. 8, he can announce his own death' (Jones 2020: 99).

Randolph Stow completed the libretto very soon after this initial contact and Hart immediately started improvising and recording versions of some of the text which he sent to Maxwell Davies, dated 2 January 1969. Although these tapes served as a point of departure for the composer in his composition, in an interview with Anne-May Krüger, Maxwell Davies relativised their direct impact on his composition:

> I don't think much. I just listened to them and he was there and I could take down what he was doing on paper and I remembered very well. And I had him, as he were, in my ear, in my head all the time I was composing.
>
> (Krüger 2014: 25)

There followed a period of rehearsals with the Pierrot Players, an ensemble of six musicians: flute, clarinet, percussion, piano/harpsichord, violin and cello. Roy Hart devoted intense periods of study to this work, aided by his wife Dorothy whose musical and piano skills were essential in helping him master the musical complexity of the score. This was to be a more theatrical piece than *Versuch über Schweine* as Hart, embodying the maddened King George III, was to interact with all the instrumentalists, each of whom were to be placed in their own silver cage, a simple but highly effective staging imagined by Richard Armstrong from Roy Hart Theatre. Armstrong also designed the costumes. Hart wore a richly embroidered, ample robe that trailed behind him, a white ruff on his chest and a soft crown that matched his robes. (Armstrong would perform this role himself with great success in the United States and Canada almost thirty-two years later.)

The premiere took place (as had *Versuch über Schweine*) in the Queen Elizabeth Hall, London on 22 April 1969. The atmosphere in the packed concert hall was feverish with excitement. Paul Silber recounts:

> One sensed the audience appreciating the whole ambiance. Then disaster struck. I was paralysed with helplessness when I saw what was going to happen. Roy was singing, indeed just like a bird, moving between one musician and the next, when, not seeing the chasm in front of him, he fell right into it. Fortunately it was only a drop of one and a half metres and he had fallen on his feet but still he had hit his side on the sharp edge of the rostrum. He was

> clearly shaken but like the incredible artist that he was, he kept going without the slightest pause. He included his shock and pain, singing it out in a truly remarkable performance and I do not think most of the audience were aware of any problem ... It was later established that he had in fact cracked three ribs. When I told him that I had seen it coming and had been unable to do anything about it, he replied typically 'Well, why didn't you call out "Watch out, Roy, you're going to fall!" before it was too late!!' For me, this performance had been an excellent demonstration of one of Roy's primary lessons in theatre 'Include it, whatever'.
>
> (Silber and Silber 2000)

The audience response was a mixture of jubilation and horror. The majority, after the initial surprise, were subjugated by the effect of Davies's richly orchestrated music that punctuated the eight scenes, and the astonishing vocal performance of Hart. The theatrical juxtaposition of each musician in their own cages with the King wandering between them, interrogating his 'bullfinches' and finally smashing the violin, was disturbing but also mesmerising. Hart's unworldly vocalisations stretched the boundaries of the real and the imagined, creating a visceral reflex in the onlooker. The critics were on the whole positive despite initial hesitation. William Mann wrote in *The Times*:

> Some of the huge audience protested vociferously. At first I thought the *Songs* inclined to dawdle: but on the whole there was plenty of contrast in pace and texture and interest. The piece is meant to have a nerve-wracking effect, and does so. It also discloses many disturbing, moving, facets of musical expression. And Mr. Hart's performance is truly extraordinary.
>
> (Mann 1969)

Desmond Shawe-Taylor of the *Sunday Times* affirmed: 'sung over a compass of some five octaves with astonishing virtuosity by that extraordinary performer Roy Hart ... the late Alfred Wolfsohn's theories of vocal extension have at last found their perfect use' (Shawe-Taylor 1969). Clearly *Eight Songs for a Mad King* had triggered an enthusiastic reaction in both the public and the critics. Maxwell Davies had succeeded in composing a tight music theatre performance that was to be a defining moment in the development of that genre. In 'Alternative Vocalities: Listening Awry to Peter Maxwell Davies's *Eight Songs for a Mad King*', Adrian Curtin underlines this:

> *Eight Songs* is an acknowledged classic of the mid-to-late twentieth century avant-garde. It is thought to have established music theatre as a credible and provocative new genre (or pseudo-genre) that subverted and redeployed existing performance conventions.
>
> (Curtin 2009: 102)

Peter Maxwell Davies himself acknowledged in a radio interview over 30 years later the remarkable longevity of *Eight Songs* and how he came to write it in the first place:

> There was this wonderful actor from South Africa called Roy Hart. [...] This Roy Hart ran a vocal group who did these multi-phonics at a place in Hampstead called the Abraxas Club. It was all very much of the period, these people writhed around on the floor singing these extraordinary harmonics. [...] Roy Hart was the first soloist in this piece and he could do these multi-phonics so I put them in the score never thinking that anyone would want to play this piece after he'd done it [...] It's a piece of its time.
>
> (Maxwell Davies 2014)

Eight Songs was almost immediately reprised at The York Festival, England, in June of 1969 and was met with an ovation and laudatory reviews. Tours in the autumn of that year and in spring 1970 took *Eight Songs* to Hamburg, Vienna, Rome, Royan and back to London's Queen Elizabeth Hall again. It clearly had a potentially long career ahead but clouds were looming in the relationship between Hart, Maxwell Davies and Maxwell Davies's manager.

Over 50 years later Kevin Crawford still recalls the indelible mark Hart's interpretation in both *Versuch über Schweine* and *Eights Songs for a Mad King* made on him, as he saw how his teacher and maestro actually had put his ideas and training into practice in these two contrasting but equally riveting performances: 'Every note of these pieces seemed to resonate my experience of this man, his ideas and my incipient yearning to follow in his footsteps' (Crawford 2019). Crawford reports that along with Alan Codd, a member of the company at that time, he was tasked by Roy Hart with writing on his behalf to Maxwell Davies and his manager at that time, James Murdoch. This long letter, dated 7 October 1969, laid out what Hart understood as the philosophical and psychological implications of his collaboration with Maxwell Davies and insisted that Maxwell Davies recognise his intrinsic value. It was uncompromising in its criticism of what Roy considered to be shortcomings in their appreciation of who he was and what he 'symbolized'. This also had a monetary and public relations implication: not being valued for who he was implied a depreciation of his worth and integrity. Crawford and Codd read the letter aloud to Maxwell Davies and Murdoch, much to the listeners' consternation. It prefigured the scission that, almost a year later, became inevitable.

Krüger examines some sections of *Eight Songs* to ascertain whether there is some truth in attributing a composer's role for Hart. Her findings, based on comparisons between tapes Hart recorded of his versions of Stow's libretto and the Maxwell Davies's final score, although still ongoing, indicate that, notwithstanding the fact that Maxwell Davies was clearly inspired by Hart, the composition, in terms of how he handles time and musical contrast are very much his own.

Perhaps time has now given us a perspective on the importance of Hart's role in *Eight Songs*, not so much in terms of his contribution to the composition as such, but more in terms of how he forced a reevaluation of the voice that transcended established conventions of what a voice signified. Adrian Curtin in *Alternative Vocalities* wrote:

> Roy Hart, proponent of a 'conscious schizophrenia' attained by mastery of extended voice, allows us to recognize that voice is not a phantom absence or a philosophical abstraction, but instead a malleable instrument that is socially and culturally conditioned and that can sound out a plethora of potential selves. *Eight Songs* heralds the complex nature of voice as a philosophical category, as a social, cultural and musical construction, and as a physiological and phenomenological reality. ... Davies's work composes the voice in flight and under pressure, evoking difference. The vocalist of the piece, in avoiding any single semantic frame, queers voice and makes evident a range of alternative vocalities.
> (Curtin 2009: 116)

The premiere of *Eight Songs* took place two days before his company's (then called the Roy Hart Speaker/ Singers) debut at the *Festival Mondial du Théâtre Universitaire* in Nancy, France with Euripides' *The Bacchae*. This was to be another pivotal moment in terms of international recognition and sparked off a series of tours abroad. In time this European acceptance of his work led Hart with other founder members to consider and finally enact a move to France, which had long-term consequences on the evolution of the company and on Hart's work.

Figure 1.2 Roy Hart and Karlheinz Stockhausen, image courtesy of Ivan Midderigh, RHT Photographic Archives.

However, 1969 afforded one other important musical collaboration for Roy Hart in his work exchanges and experiments with Karlheinz Stockhausen which led to Hart being invited to perform at the Fondation Maeght in Saint Paul de Vence, above Nice on 26 July. Subsequently the two men worked together at the very influential 24th *International Ferienkurse für Neue Musik* at Darmstadt on 1 September of that same year. The latter event marked the end of their working relationship. In the previous year Stockhausen had been so impressed by Roy Hart's voice on tape that he had written: 'After having listened to your tape I wish to write to you immediately. Your technique makes possible what a few experimental composers have been seeking for several years. BRAVO!!' (Stockhausen 1968). Subsequently Stockhausen visited The Abraxas Club studio where he witnessed a rehearsal of *The Bacchae* and discussed his future collaboration with Hart. Stockhausen didn't compose specifically for Roy Hart's voice. Hart participated in *Spirale* on 26 July 1969 at the Fondation Maeght, Saint Paul de Vence, France and in a section called *Abwarts* from the *Aus den Sieben Tagen* cycle at the Beethovensalle, Darmnstadt, Germany in September of the same year. *Spiral* was more structured: its starting point being the aleatory sounds emitted by short-wave radio, which were then manipulated, echoed and transformed by the performers according to a series of signs Stockhausen invented: a kind of controlled improvisation. It consisted of 206 events, only some of which were performed on each occasion. A subsequent review described the work as an:

> electronic version, vocal version (with the stunning Roy Hart) ... We climb up the bleachers to our places in shadow, amongst squeaky, scratchy sounds, paroxysms. These accumulate, growing, multiplying like storm clouds, to a summit that is breath taking, and then freeze hard.
>
> (Cadieu 1969)

Aus Den Sieben Tagen, however, was a further step on Stockhausen's journey towards what he called intuitive music and required performers to respond to a series of written instructions, semi-poetic in substance, allowing for much individual choice and improvisation. It was following the performance in Darmstadt that differences emerged between Hart, Stockhausen and some of the other musicians. Although Hart had impressed the public and the critics with his vocal and acting skills, he had infuriated Stockhausen, most probably by going beyond what Stockhausen and his musicians would have expected from a singer who had only just begun to work with them. 'The composer went so far as to stage a mock trial after the performance with the audience as jury, the charge being that Roy was guilty of treason to the arts' (Pikes 2019: 102).

The reviewer for the *Darmstadter Echo* described the conflict in these terms:

> The quarrelsome morning makes him (Hart) timid. The public had seen him in Stockhausen's 'Abwarts' like a pouncing tiger, a magnificent performer, dancer and mime, like an actor, like a singer climbing vertically, with the voice of an orangutan—he balances on the line of demarcation between his intuition and Stockhausen's fixed score, which after all is not so flexible as all that, and needs to finish in discordant sound. Here are two worlds: the human of Hart, and the mechanical of Stockhausen. Hart thinks that they could have found a bridge, if they had had a clarifying rehearsal before the performance.
>
> (*Darmstadter Echo* 1969)

Be that as it may, Hart rarely spoke about his experiences in Darmstadt, but Stockhausen bore him no ill, and sent him a warm note afterwards.

In January 1971 at the Festival 'Art Vocal et Musique de Notre Temps' in Royan, France, Roy Hart and Roy Hart Theatre performed a double bill. In the first half of the evening Roy Hart premiered a new musical work written for him by Michael Vetter with Vetter playing recorder and Karlheinz Boettger on guitar. For the second part of the evening Roy Hart Theatre presented *Nexus*, directed by Anna Allen. In 1972 he recorded *La Peste* (*The Plague*) by Antonin Artaud with jazz pianist George Grüntz, for West Deutsche Rundfunk in Cologne, directed by Paul Pörtner. Hart also worked with the French composer Andre Almuro on *Visit to Godenhall*, recorded in December 1972 for ORTF (French National Radio).

In 1972 the last two pieces that were specifically composed for Roy Hart were produced. The first, *Beschreibung der Inneren Erfahrungen* (*Descriptions of an Inner Experience*) by young Austrian composer Meinhard Rudenauer, was presented on Austrian radio on 17 January as part of the *Internationale Gesellschaft für Neue Musik* (International Society for New Music). This piece drew on visits Rudenauer made to the Hart studio in London, and pitted the voice against five instruments – clarinet, tenor trombone, viola, cello and piano – until finally achieving a complete blending of the instrumental and vocal sound. No words were spoken in this piece. The voice appeared as a sheer presence in sound, in timbre, and in dynamic contrast to the instrumental forces. Unfortunately, the piece was not performed again, but a recording still exists in the Roy Hart Theatre archive.

In summer of the same year, 1972, Roy Hart and the company took part in a large-scale musical experiment entitled *Kyrie Eleison* in Saint Pancras Church, London under the direction of Vladimir Rodzianko, a Russian composer. *Kyrie Eleison* was an audacious experiment in music which brought together four company soloists – Roy Hart, Dorothy Hart, Vivienne Young and Robert Harvey – with a full chorus of the company and musicians from the professional music group Music Plus. Specially created for the cavernous space of Saint Pancras Church in central London it contrasted composed extended-range songs for the vocalists with aleatoric or random entrances from chorus and musicians based on cues from huge mobiles that spun from the beams of the church. The four soloists could move freely underneath the mobiles, hanging from the ceiling, that spiralled around in the convective air currents in the church. Each mobile had several 'faces'. The chorus of singers and musicians took their cues from the random or chance rotations of the mobiles. The soloists' vocal lines were demanding and intricate: the chorus chanted variations on the theme *Kyrie Eleison*, while the musicians played themes and orchestrations suggested by the mobiles. This performance was shown on several occasions and was one of the rare moments when Hart and all the company performed together in

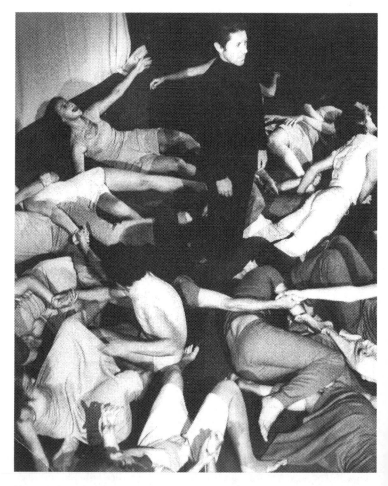

Figure 1.3 Roy Hart with Roy Hart Company performing *Kyrie Eleison*, St. Pancras Church, London, image courtesy of Ivan Midderigh, RHT Photographic Archives.

that year. It also marked the last time Hart collaborated with a composer from outside the company. Henceforth he preferred to draw on the musical resources within the company, and turned his attention to developing pieces where he would perform with Roy Hart Theatre.

THE ABRAXAS CLUB: THE BIRTH OF ROY HART THEATRE (1967-74)

By late 1967, Roy Hart and his group were on the threshold of a new chapter in their lives. Predominantly younger people had joined the group recently, bringing a greater diversity of talent and social origins to the ensemble. This group, now almost 30 strong, had started workshopping intensively their version of *The Bacchae* under Hart's direction. Hart and the group now had the aim of testing out the validity of their approach, and exposing it to a wider public. Roy Hart was shifting away from private teaching (now assumed by senior members of the group), and this allowed him to concentrate more on his own vocal development, with a view to making recordings that might attract composers interested in writing for him. Moreover, he was able to focus his energies on the intense studio phase of developing his version of *The Bacchae*. A phase that was to span almost three years before its first performances in April 1969.

Hart realised that his group had now outgrown the rather small studio space he had created in a living room at The Ridgeway. He needed to expand his workspace in order to accommodate the increasing number of students, especially as he was beginning to introduce bodywork and dance into the skill base and movement exploration of the group. Frenkel and Monty Crawford were instrumental in facilitating this new phase in Hart's professional life, which enabled him and his group to realise their potential as performers and create the solid basis for a company. Thanks to their business skills and philanthropy, The Hampstead Squash Club in Belsize Park, London was identified as being a potential location to create a centre for the group's activities. The club, which was a traditional feature of Belsize Park, offered only a basic membership for the use of its squash courts, and it was now for sale. Hart's idea was to transform it into a much more dynamic centre, offering not only squash courts but also a gymnasium, dance classes, bar/restaurant, massage and osteopathy. The changing rooms were renovated with the addition of saunas, a hairdressing salon was even added on later. Most importantly for Roy Hart, there was a state-of-the-art soundproofed studio occupying most of the top floor where he could conduct his meetings and rehearsals or retire for his own personal vocal research and rehearsal.

Hart named the club The Abraxas Club in honour of the Gnostic God Abraxas who symbolised for Hart the creative synthesis of opposites. Hart probably met this God through his readings of C.G. Jung's *Seven Sermons to the Dead*, a series of seven poetic visions, that had inspired Jung throughout his life, although Abraxas also appears in the writings of Herman Hesse and Miguel Serrano. In 1966 Serrano had published *C.G. Jung and Herman Hesse A record of Two Friendships*. In this book Serrano quotes Herman Hesse: 'Our God is named Abraxas, and he is both God and the Devil at the same time. You will find in him both the world of light and the shadows' (Serrano 1966: 6). Hart realized that Abraxas stood for the very principles he had been working with in his voice: the bringing together of the beautiful and the ugly, order and disorder, height and depth, the spiritual and the sexual. This in turn had led him to interrogate conventions and assumptions in social life and relationships. Finally, he had found a symbol that suited his view of art and life: unity in contradiction, something coming out of nothing. Hart was not the only influential practitioner to be engaged with similar principles in the 1960s. Jerzy Grotowski had identified two fundamental equations in his work: the *conjunctio oppositorum* (conjunction of opposites) and the *via negativa* (way of negation). He too searched for an act of 'Total Theatre' that embraced both the personal and cultural heritage of his actors.

The move from The Ridgeway to the newly born Abraxas Club was celebrated mid-October 1968, and it did indeed herald a renewed period of activity and creativity within the company. Hart had a state-of-the-art studio at his disposition, almost three times bigger than the studio at The Ridgeway: sufficient to receive the by now burgeoning numbers of those who were working with him on a regular basis, as well as an increasing number of guests from a wide cross-section of artists, performers, creators, writers and scientists. The club's facilities were quickly taken advantage of by the members of his group: dance classes with Robert Harvey, Barrie Irwin or Derek Rossignol were regular features, taking place not only in the dance studio but sometimes in the early morning on the squash courts which were only used by members from 9am onwards. Guest dance teachers gave classes, mainly Martha Graham Technique with Shelley Lee, open to the public, that Hart's group also participated in. Hart invited Hebe Rosa, a highly influential teacher of modern dance from Montevideo, to teach over an extended period the rapidly forming company. The club also housed a generous bar and restaurant facilities. These became the focus for weekly cabaret performances by company members, subsequently to be renamed 'Cathédrales', and were largely hosted and inspired by Paul Silber and Barrie Irwin with Hart's blessing. These regular events gave the company members an opportunity to try out a range of performance styles: from farce to musical theatre, from vocal performance to experimental movement. The material was almost exclusively structured by the company, Hart limiting his engagement to that of observer and sometime critic. Many of these scenes and mini-performances were to be further developed and were included in, or, in some cases, generated future works for the company.

By the time The Abraxas Club opened its doors Hart had already started work on *The Bacchae* by Euripides using Phillip Vellacott's translation. Some of its scenes were the object of intense improvisation, but Hart insisted that all the participants learn all the text by heart even if they did not have a named role. Although some members of the group were assigned specific roles, no one was excluded. The chorus was omnipresent throughout the piece and all the actors were onstage throughout. To some degree this came about because the studio at The Abraxas Club had no wings or exits (except the entrance door), so every person in the room was always present. The bigger studio enabled Hart to invite many of the Hampstead artistic and literary communities who frequented the club to watch rehearsals and presentations, including Harold Pinter, George Steiner and Steven Berkoff. Frank Marcus reviewed a rehearsal in December 1968 for *The Sunday Telegraph*:

> Above all the falsetto wheezes, cracked roars, *glissando* swoops and choral incantations conjured up the ghost of Artaud: the prophet of unreason. Mr Hart has welded together a group of disparate individuals into a single body: their limbs intermingled like the tentacles of an octopus; the voices belonged to all. In an atmosphere of sectarian intensity Mr Hart exercised the twenty-headed monster of his creation. It was an enthralling but slightly menacing experience.
> (Marcus 1968)

The first three months of 1969 were a particularly intense period for Hart and his group, as Hart was to premiere *Versuch über Schweine* in February, prepare the *Eight Songs for a Mad King* for its April premiere and rehearse

The Bacchae. This period reached a climax in spring 1969 when Hart's performers, now called the Roy Hart Speaker/Singers, were invited to the World University Theatre Festival of Nancy, France, to perform their version of *The Bacchae*, just several days after Hart was to perform the solo role in *Eight Songs for a Mad King* at the Queen Elizabeth Hall.

By the autumn of 1969, Hart and his group had renamed themselves again and were now, after much discussion and hesitation on Hart's part, Roy Hart Theatre. The company was invited to perform revised versions of *The Bacchae* at both The Place and The Roundhouse of London, while Hart was also now touring with *Eight Songs for a Mad King*. Slowly a change was coming over the organisation of the company and Roy Hart's directing role within it. Members were encouraged to start producing their own work, often under the mentorship of Hart, but with a lot of freedom to experiment and stage their own talents and interests. This resulted in a series of minor and major productions (some of which are reviewed more extensively in **Chapter Three**). The subsequent addition of a large rehearsal space on the ground floor offered company members facilities for further expansion.

In the early 1970s the company took three long summer holidays together, twice in the former Yugoslavia on the island of Stara Baška and once on the Greek island of Paxos off Corfu. These experiences had welded the company even closer together and served as a model for living as a community. Gradually, once they were back in London, some company members gave up their individual or small flats and moved into The Abraxas Club, occupying studios and other spaces at night that had to be vacated for their scheduled daytime activities. This proved to be a preparation for its eventual relocation to France and a communal lifestyle.

From 1970 to early 1973 Hart concentrated on his career as a soloist in works we have cited above. Occasionally he would still accompany Roy Hart Theatre on international tours, performing as a soloist before the company appeared onstage. Hart used several vehicles for this. For the Maison de la Culture of Rennes, France in June 1970 he sung and improvised with the soundtrack of *Eight Songs for a Mad King* before Roy Hart Theatre performed *The Song of Everest*.

As well as his musical projects, Hart continued to search for writers capable of inventing texts centred on his and the company's expanded vocal skills. Already In 1965 English poet Peter Redgrove had written *The Case*, a long poetic oratory dedicated to Hart, which Hart recorded with the aim of having it broadcast by the BBC, but unfortunately, this project was rejected. Other times he used existing texts: a medieval poem called *Athelgar* and *A Memorable Fantasy* by William Blake or a piece of contemporary writing by Christopher Mann. These were the object of intense study by Hart and the company and were faithfully recorded. However, above all, he wanted to engage with writers capable of seizing the potential that he and his company offered. And he looked for authors of a similar mindset to his own. In meeting Serge Béhar, a doctor of Turkish Sephardic origin now living in Paris, Hart felt that he had finally met someone who could do just this. Béhar was already a well-recognised playwright in France, and he agreed to give Hart *Mariage de Lux*, that he had written previously, but allowed Hart carte blanche to adapt it to meet his and the company's requirements. Béhar subsequently wrote a substantial solo piece, *Biodrame*, specifically for Hart's voice. Hart performed *Biodrame* frequently from 1972, sometimes alone as part of a demonstration or lecture/presentation, sometimes as an 'opener' for performances by the company. It was a tour de force vocally and verbally, and in a sense became a 'live' visiting card for him (see **Chapter Three** for fuller details of this and other productions).

From 1970 onwards Hart also began to teach in university and conservatory contexts in France and Spain. In France he taught at CUIFERD, the Centre for Theatre Research at the University of Nancy linked to the World Student Festival, and later in Madrid at the *Escuela Superior de Arte Dramático* at the invitation of José Monleón. These workshops were the object of intense interest from the theatrical profession, and were reviewed in national newspapers. In Spain, in particular, responses to both Hart's teaching and to performances by the company were very enthusiastic. Hart returned to Barcelona to teach in February 1973 at the *Instituto de Teatro de Barcelona*. Later teaching engagements were then taken over by senior members of the troupe, Richard Armstrong and Barrie Irwin at the *Escuela Superior*, Vivienne Young and Elizabeth (Liza) Mayer with the *Pequeno Teatro* in Madrid. Hart also presented his work at various international congresses during this time including Vienna (5th International Congress of Psychodrama) in 1968, Prague (Demonstration/lecture at Psychiatric Clinic of Professor Voudiaček) in 1970, Zagreb (6th International Congress of Psychodrama) in 1970, and Tokyo (7th International Congress of Psychodrama) in 1972.

As well as performing *Biodrame* in Europe in 1973, Hart began to develop a collaboration with the German writer Paul Pörtner, who was interested in extending the bounds of textual expression. Hart had already worked with Pörtner for West Deutsche Rundfunk on a project with the jazz musician George Grünz based on a lesser-known text of Antonin Artaud, *Il n'y a plus de firmament*. Pörtner reworked an earlier poem, newly named *Ich Bin*, for Hart and the company as a vehicle for them to explore using their vocal and movement skills. The piece was highly impressionistic, more in the nature of a sound poem than any narrative sequence, although it did roughly sketch the journey to self-realisation of the individual 'I'. Hart invited a small number of actors from the company to explore this piece, mainly through improvisation. In these rehearsals Hart engaged in intense physical interaction with the other actors in a way that he had not done previously. This marked a profound desire on his part to integrate himself as a performer into the company, and experience directly the very discipline and imaginative theatre-making skills he had coached up to that point. Using the rough parable of the poem, they improvised intensively over several months. Hart rose to this challenge, engaging himself completely in the physical and vocal struggles with the other actors. This was probably the closest he came to embedding himself unreservedly in a performance, although only short extracts of these improvisations were to find their way into subsequent public performances. In the same time period Roy asked Robert Harvey to choreograph a short ballet for himself and several members of the company. This was based on *Namouna*, ballet music written by Edouard Lalo. Again, this was an important step for Hart, who had always felt shy about his body and his own dancing skills. By engaging with other members of the company, he too submitted to direction, and allowed himself to explore this relatively undeveloped side of himself. This immersion in dance was to come in useful later for scenes in *L'Economiste,* the final work produced under his direction (this production is considered closely in **Chapter Three**).

By October 1973 Hart and the company had *Biodrame*, *Ich Bin* and *Mariage de Lux* in their repertoire, which were three pieces that had been either specifically written for or remodelled for Hart and the company. Hart decided to put these three pieces together under the title *Three Moods* and presented them at The Cockpit Theatre, London and in the following year at The Open Space, London. It was not received enthusiastically. Two of the pieces were in French and one in German. All three were performed in an expressionist manner with little modification for an English-speaking audience: no subtitles, no sections in English and limited stage notes. One play would shift into another and back again with little effort to discriminate between the three works. Much attention was given to the plastic and choreographic aspects of the performance, and the vocal and verbal expression was orchestrated, almost operatic in sections. *Three Moods* signalled Hart's increasing wish to distance himself from the English theatre scene and engage even more fully in the countries that had responded positively to his work: France, Spain and Switzerland.

By late 1973, having already intimated he wished to leave London in response to the critical reception of the company's recent work, Hart looked to establish a new centre for the company somewhere in mainland Europe where he felt there was more understanding and support of his work. After the holiday on Paxos, Greece, different teams searched for a suitable property, but to no avail.

L'ECONOMISTE AND MALÉRARGUES (1974–5)

However, Vivienne Young, Lucienne Deschamps and Monty Crawford made one last unplanned visit to the then remote Cévennes area of France where they happened upon an entire hamlet, called Malérargues: it comprised a very large stone building officially called a chateau, which was surrounded by multiple outbuildings and land. It offered the living and studio spaces that could accommodate the company which had now expanded to almost 50 people. The property had been abandoned for some time and desperately needed renovation. Monty Crawford (father of Kevin Crawford), assisted by Lucienne Deschamps and Gabriel Riversmore, negotiated the acquisition. In summer 1974 a pioneer group of seven members took the lengthy train ride from London to Alès, and commenced the daunting task of rebuilding and preparing for the arrival of the remainder of the company which was phased over the next eight months.

This departure marked a new disparate phase in the company's life. Roy Hart gathered a group of his closest collaborators around him and they occupied a chalet belonging to Louis Frenkel in Anzère, Switzerland. A larger group remained in London, still running The Abraxas Club, which by then was up for sale, and prepared for the imminent departure for France. The third group were already in France. Between these three groups there was a steady stream of letters and phone calls and occasional visits.

In late 1974 Serge Béhar finally gave Hart the play he had been requesting from him for some time. This was to be a play for the company and himself that would allow Hart to enunciate his philosophy in a theatrical form. However, Béhar's first offering was judged unsatisfactory: the play was neither written specifically for the company nor did it convey the kind of message Hart wanted. After meetings with Béhar in Paris, Roy Hart and the group in Anzère began to engage in a lengthy process of rewriting and communicating with him, with the support and input from company members in London and Malérargues. In January of 1975, Béhar delivered a final version to the company that was satisfactory to Hart and his closest collaborators. In honour of the fact that the rewriting had involved not only Serge, and the group closest to Hart, but also members of the company who had remained in London, and the pioneer group of seven who had arrived early in Malérargues, Hart proposed that the play, now titled *L'Economiste*, be presented as a 'Collective Creation of Roy Hart Theatre inspired by a text of Serge Béhar'.

In late January of 1975, Hart and his circle of collaborators arrived in Malérargues to commence rehearsals amidst a living and financial situation which, to say the least, was precarious. The buildings were still undergoing substantial renovation. Only one studio was in operation; heating, kitchen duties, sanitary conditions and finances were all challenging. Gradually new arrivals were integrated into the rehearsals and *L'Economiste* began to take flesh. It was an ambitious production engaging a large cast of nineteen performers and six musicians and required intense hours of rehearsal to achieve the kind of coordination of text, sound, music and choreography that Hart envisioned.

A preview at the Chapelle des Pénitents Blancs in Alès in March 1975 preceded the premiere at the Cratère, the main theatre in Alès on 12 April. Rehearsals continued after that event right up to the company's departure for extensive tours in Austria and Spain at the end of April. Throughout the first fortnight of May, performances in Austria were accompanied by workshops and conferences. The reception to the new piece was mixed. There was some undoubted excitement and enthusiasm, but also some criticism, not so much of the play but of the nature of the group that Hart had formed and of his influence and role. On 17 May, Hart, Dorothy Hart, Vivienne Young and Paul Silber left by car, a BMW, for the next leg of the tour, that would eventually take them to Spain, and they stopped for a night in the hills above Nice. The rest of the company left the next day by train, and stopped for the night in a hotel in Nice. During that night they were awoken with the shattering news that Roy Hart, Dorothy Hart and Vivienne Young had been killed in a car accident earlier that day while driving on the motorway not far from Fréjus in Provence, France. The company, shocked and deeply grieving, assembled in a hotel room, and were collected in the morning by a coach chartered from Malérargues. Roy Hart Theatre, now without its titular head, had, in addition to recovering from its terrible loss, the immense challenge of reinventing itself.

Roy Hart, Dorothy Hart and Vivienne Young's remains were repatriated to Malérargues and buried on a terrace overlooking the property. Company member Enrique Pardo describes the enormity of the loss:

> We had lost our 'guru' and didn't know what to do. We had actually just signed the purchase of this place [Malérargues] and withdrew back into it after 'the accident'. This was a blessing in some ways, a refuge, but, in others, a traumatic reaction of mourning and isolation. Without the 'leaden' anchoring of that property, I think we would have breathed deeply and each gone her or his ways. Malérargues, in a way, held the group together.
>
> (Pardo 2019)

Paul Silber, who miraculously survived the accident recalls:

> Within two weeks of my return to Malérargues, we were again rehearsing *L'Economiste*. What possessed us to do this I cannot imagine. For us to have attempted to insert our own little selves into the places of those, our lost giants of theatre, was an act of the greatest possible folly. However, this is what we insisted on doing.
>
> (Silber 2020)

L'Economiste was remounted with Elizabeth (Liza) Mayer, Lucienne Deschamps and Richard Armstrong assuming the roles of Vivienne Young, Dorothy Hart and Roy Hart. Paul Silber played the Technarch, a role previously assumed by Armstrong. The overall structure and direction of the play remained intact although Mayer, Deschamps and Armstrong moulded the central characters of Flora, Justine and Maurice to their own style. The premiere of this revised version took place on 13 August in the local village hall at Saint Jean du Gard, and was followed in October by a performance in Alès. In the spring of 1976 this new version of *L'Economiste* toured Spain extensively before returning to perform in Nîmes in May of that year. But astonishingly enough, that was not the only project that retained the attention of the company despite its immense loss and its organisational and financial issues.

Two lighter, more flexible performances called *L'Enthousiasme* and *L'Enchanté*, collages of songs, dances and choral chants, were designed for touring the small villages and hamlets of the Cévennes area close to Malérargues for the summer of 1975 and 1976. The remaking of *L'Economiste* for international touring and the birth of *L'Enthousiasme* and *L'Enchanté* for local tours marked the extraordinary dedication of a company that, in spite of all, was committed to its new home in France and was determined to make its way both abroad and regionally. Roy Hart Theatre continued as a professional troupe for the next 15 years, creating over 20 works, some earning national and international recognition. These included a French language version of Shakespeare's *Tempest* (1977), *Furies* (1986) in coproduction with The Talking Band, New York, and *Pagliacci* (1985) directed by Richard Armstrong, performed at LA MAMA, New York (which earned an OBIE Award that honours the highest calibre of off-Broadway and off-off-Broadway theatre to recognize brave work, champion new material and advance careers in theatre). Other productions included *Kaspar* (1984) directed by Johannes Theron in Paris (which won The Prix Charles Dullin, an annual prize awarded to the production that shows most promise and achievement), and *Moby Dick* (1989) directed by Linda Wise at the *Printemps des Comèdiens* festival, Montpellier (which won the Prix Jean Vilar, awarded for a performance that distinguished itself during the festival).

The company toured extensively in South America and Europe, enjoying a period of sustained support from French regional and national bodies that support culture. As the years passed members of the company began to assert their own research and artistic pathways, and in some cases created their own companies. Pantheatre, created by Enrique Pardo, Liza Mayer and Linda Wise, was the first company to take this route followed closely by Archipelago, directed by Johannes Theron and Rafael Lopez Barrantes. Also, in 1990, later Roy Hart Theatre Company members Flavio Polizzy and Renata Roagna formed the company Amadée in Montpellier which produced work in the region for almost 20 years. Other companies that evolved from Roy Hart Theatre include Pascale Ben's La Voix Est Libre and David Goldsworthy's Dia Pasôn, both in southern France.

From 1981 to 1990 Roy Hart Theatre continued to extend its repertoire of performances, from original music pieces like *Musique pour Marsyas* directed by Boris Moore to solo works including *Prévert et Moi*, performed and directed by Robert Harvey. By 1990 Roy Hart Theatre company ceased producing its own works and in 1991 the Roy Hart International Artistic Centre (*Centre Artistique International Roy Hart* – CAIRH) was born in order to sustain the legacy of Wolfsohn, Hart and Roy Hart Theatre in Malérargues.

WHO WAS ROY HART?

Kevin Crawford remembers: *Roy Hart was of a medium height, built very stockily, with a wide neck and chiselled features. His legs were wide in girth but well-muscled. Overall, he gave an impression of immense physical power, but an almost relaxed manner belied that strength. His light brown hair, when I knew him, was thinning and his teeth showed signs of extensive dental treatment. A gap between his two upper front teeth was a distinctive feature. He had already taken up using contact lenses. He loved eating well and liked to travel, discovering restaurants and hotels that he would revisit. He emanated an extraordinary warmth, but could be cold if he considered you had transgressed. He had surrounded himself with a group of incredible diversity and had an uncanny knack in bringing the best out in them. He believed in the fundamental importance of human relationships, which he called the 'I-Thou' principle. Being in his presence was always a moment-to-moment experience, a sense of living life to the fullest, be it playing a game of squash, drinking tea, scrutinising a newspaper article or diving into the heart-stopping depths of a rehearsal.*

Hart was in many ways a complex and apparently contradictory personality: intensely committed to what he considered his mission, the dissemination of what he called an 'Eight octave approach to life' and yet anchored in steadfast loyalty to his company. He had renounced his early ambition to be a famous actor in order, almost monk-like, to follow the teachings and vision of Wolfsohn for 15 years. Even once he took over the leadership after Wolfsohn's death, his sights were channelled away from his own performance potential towards teaching and building a group of people who were committed in a long-term way to the vocal and personal research he offered. By the end of the 1960s, as the founder members matured, Hart felt he had established his 'school' and that he could turn to what had been his heart's desire: to make theatre, both as a soloist and as a director of an ensemble-based company. His rise to fame was meteoric as composer after composer realised what his presence and extraordinary vocal gifts had to offer. But even this success was to be rejected, as he felt that his integrity was not being respected by most of the composers. This must have been a bitter blow given his love of performance. However, his search for kindred spirits did lead him to writers who created texts which were specially conceived for him or the company. As Hart's company grew in size, he gradually relinquished authority, teaching duties and artistic competence to other members. But as the group grew so did the complexity of relations within it, including his own with Dorothy Hart and Vivienne Young.

Hart, as his early teachers at RADA had noted, had often found criticism difficult to swallow, and yet he longed to be accepted by the theatre profession, if it was on his terms … Although he would rebuff accusations of being a manipulator or engendering a cult-like activity, he would be deeply affected by such claims, which put into question the integrity of his work. Hart, as we see in **Chapter Two**, *wrote little about his work and absolutely nothing about the concrete nature of his teaching. But I do believe that he wrote a 'book' in each of the members of his troupe, and that this book has been carried forward by them, filtered through their own individuality, and thus transmitted and disseminated to successive generations of practitioners. Hart's heritage was an oral one, imprinted in the cells and memory of those who worked with him. His voice, like Orpheus, does come down to us, through their tongues.*

2

ROY HART AND DOROTHY HART

Writings, interviews, letters

INTRODUCTION

Roy Hart has left us little written trace of his work, life and ideas. Two papers delivered to congresses on psychodrama and psychotherapy constitute the longest pieces of writing that Hart undertook, and these give us an insight into how he conceived his work and, at that time, his unique position at the junction between the extension of the voice, psychology and theatre. They give us a glimpse into how Hart believed the human voice was an essential tool for opening up the personality and promoting social and cultural consciousness. Apart from these two papers, Hart often wrote, almost always by hand, messages and letters to those close to him that reveal facets of himself and throw light on his beliefs and decisions. These messages often took place in the context of lengthy letter exchanges with members of the company. These exchanges covered a range of topics, from dreams to personal relationships, from commentary on articles read in studio meetings to organisational issues regarding the running of the company to artistic projects. In a predigital world, where telephones were not yet as ubiquitous as they were to become, letters, drawings, paintings and poems created a constant flow of communication. In addition, he wrote letters to fellow artists, scientists and administrators, often with the collaboration of Dorothy Hart, Vivienne Young, Elizabeth [Liza] Mayer and others. These letters also tell their story: sometimes of closeness in spirit, sometimes conflictual or confrontational. Dorothy Hart, in particular, played a pivotal role in articulating Hart's conception of theatre as evidenced in the company's production of *The Bacchae* and *L'Economiste*. These documents constitute a body of written material that traces Hart's emergence as the leading proponent of Alfred Wolfsohn's work on the voice until his death in 1975. Roy Hart was, however, more at home with speaking aloud his thoughts, responses and convictions. These were shared in an almost daily dialogue with those close to him and, in particular, in regular meetings with his company as well as in private exchanges. Little of this has been recorded but interviews with founder members of the company and a few short recordings do give the flavour and gist of his presence and perceptiveness. An annotated script of *Biodrame* throws light on his own process as an actor. Finally, Roy Hart was interviewed extensively on several occasions, in particular by José Monleón, Pepe Estruch and Ricardo Domenech for *Primer Acto* in January 1972. The interviews resulted from a series of meetings organised by *Primer Acto*, Spain's foremost theatre magazine in March 1971 during a season of workshops that Hart directed at the Escuela Superior de Arte Dramático of Madrid. These interviews provide a valuable addition to our knowledge of him and his definition of his work.

WRITINGS

HOW A VOICE GAVE ME A CONSCIENCE

In August 1967, five years after inheriting the direction of the work on the voice from Wolfsohn, Hart delivered a paper to the 7th International Congress for Psychotherapy in Wiesbaden, Germany. It was entitled 'How a Voice Gave Me a Conscience' (Roy Hart 1967).

To open, Roy Hart states:

> Twenty years ago I started a dedicated study of the human voice. Today I find that I am the head of a group of some thirty people who form a kind of synthetic, growing family. The story of this organic growth is, I think, very relevant to the theme of this Congress: the relationship of society to man, and the role of creative Art as preventative medicine.
>
> (Roy Hart 1967)

Hart speaks about the heterogeneous make-up of the members of this synthetic family:

> Most of these people were not naturally gregarious or prone to follow a leader: yet they chose to subject themselves to each other and (as some at first thought) to me, but, in fact, both they and I are subject to the creative research work we do – to the principle of an eight octave voice. Eight-octave? Yes. We find that any normal human voice, male or female, usually reckoned to have a range of from two to two and a half octaves, may be extended, by training, to six or more octaves, gaining in expressiveness and emotional content in the process. This cultural-philosophical system of voice-training is an empirical lay activity, which has already been observed by medical specialists for its therapeutic value in the treatment of neurosis, and for its remarkable scientific aspects, in the field of the extension of vocal function. However, to my mind, its most interesting aspect is the emergence of genuine family relationships and of a growing social awareness among those who adhere to this work.
>
> (Roy Hart 1967)

In these few sentences Roy Hart lays out the fundamentals that underpin his work: his synthetic family, but also himself, are 'subject to the creative work we do – to the principle of the eight -octave voice'. The human voice can be extended thus 'gaining in expressiveness and emotional content'. His approach is based on a 'cultural-philosophical system of voice-training'. Above all he notes: 'its most interesting aspect is the emergence of genuine family relationships and of a growing social awareness' (Roy Hart 1967).

Hart then recounts his personal journey:

> Yet I had known for some time that my voice was not rooted, not literally embodied; that the varied roles I was considered to perform so well were actually only figments of my imagination with no connection with my body. In personal relationships I was an aloof outsider. On leaving R.A.D.A., I was immediately offered a most promising opening in the Theatre. I thought I was dedicated to the Theatre, and my friends forecast a brilliant future. Yet, at this point, where personal ambition might have been expected to take over, I made an extraordinary choice. I turned down the proffered 'big chance' in order to research into the nature and meaning of the human voice.
>
> (Roy Hart 1967)

This 'extraordinary choice', coupled with his meeting with Wolfsohn, changed the course of his life, determining his interest in the relationship between the mind and the body, with the voice as key to this relationship.

Once he had completed his acting studies at RADA, Hart decided to devote himself entirely to the research with Wolfsohn. His interest became focused on 'the relationship between the actor and his personal life. I became concerned with the relationship between voice and personality, especially as this manifested itself in a spectrum of energy production varying from apathy to intensity' (ibid.). He found that the work had profound effects on people's personal lives. After Wolfsohn's death, the role of leader was thrust upon Roy Hart by Wolfsohn's pupils and by people outside that circle, as he was considered the student closest to Wolfsohn and the one who had most assimilated his teaching and ideas: 'I had thought of myself as an artist, an actor in the making. But because I took that Art deadly seriously, it had led me elsewhere. This is the hub of my whole thesis' (Roy Hart 1967).

At this point in the paper Hart describes how he defined singing in the context of his work:

> For singing, as we practice it, is literally the resurrection or redemption of the body. The capacity to 'hold' the voice in identification with the body makes biological reality of the concept 'I am'. The ability to hold fast with whole body in vocal production can, with correct training, develop an ability to hold fast in complex real life situations. Because I had learned to hold myself in sound, I found I was able to hold others as a leader in concentration.
>
> (Roy Hart 1967)

Hart argues that a healed society would result from the therapeutic effects of artistic expression. Following Wolfsohn's example he invents ways of developing group sensitivity and listening:

> new exercises are constantly evolving, such as listening to long stretches of silence and digesting the meaning of the wisps of human sound that emerge, or learning to orchestrate the background music to a dramatic performance by using any object within reach as a musical instrument.
>
> (Roy Hart 1967)

Hart argues that this kind of enhanced artistic expression and ability to experiment grows from a developed sensory awareness:

> Group sensitivity to atmosphere and the artistic requirements of the moment has become so developed that this kind of orchestration has often been extremely moving. Watching the language of face and body has likewise led to exercises involving minute muscular movements. Wrestling and balancing exercises are frequently used during the act of sound production.
>
> (Roy Hart 1967)

But it is clear from this paper that the artistic expression that remains at the heart of his work is predicated on a similar attention to detail and awareness in everyday life, in what amounts to a challenge to all performers to engage more fully in life outside the studio too:

> each student is trained to bring into the studio an awareness of his outside activities and relationships, and to be prepared at any moment to render these experiences in dramatic form. There is group discussion of dreams and personal problems. The dreams are often used in artistic formula, dance, drama, and painting. Every student keeps a dream record, which is filed, indexed and cross-referenced (including the children's) – a unique mine of intrapsychic material. Every student is every other student's friendly analyst.
>
> (Roy Hart 1967)

Hart speaks about 'head types' who find it easier to engage in intellectual activities like listening to articles read aloud in the studio and then analysing and commenting on them. In contrast 'tummy types' are more at home with physical and rhythmic engagement. The goal of the work is to integrate head and body, head and tummy. He also speaks to gender and gender fluidity, the terms used in the following extract might seem dated now, but the thinking is as relevant now as it was then:

> Every student is aware of a balancing principle at work alongside the breaking down of barriers. The exploring of male and female, height and depth, conscious and unconscious goes on and the hermaphroditic personality takes on many forms of imbalance before true balance is found.
>
> (Roy Hart 1967)

Hart goes on in this paper to describe the value of art in society, and how important it is to value the creativity from all persons in society – this became a fundamental touchstone of Hart's philosophy and it was expressed by the range of those who engaged with him in the company. The members of the company included business directors, television technicians, photographers, visual artists, students, journalists, as well as those who were already involved in theatre and dance. Sometimes Hart would refer to this as 'creating something out of nothing'. This was an essential part of the daily working ethic of the company, and it underpinned his belief in the hidden potential in each person.

Hart's paper closes with this affirmation:

> I firmly believe that the greatest contributing force to mental breakdown is the lack of outlet for truthful self-expression, tolerance of this expression by others and courage to persevere in it for oneself. The medium we have chosen can safely contain the variety of man's emotions without crushing him.
>
> (Roy Hart 1967)

THE OBJECTIVE VOICE

In March of 1972 Hart presented another paper, 'The Objective Voice', at the 7th International Congress for Psychodrama in Tokyo. By this time (as detailed in **Chapter One**) Hart had already collaborated with three major European composers: Maxwell Davies, Henze and Stockhausen. They had all written or adapted pieces specifically for his voice but, in each case, their artistic collaboration had subsequently foundered. At the same time Roy Hart Theatre, as his company was now called, was enjoying critical success and was about to make a significant tour throughout Europe. On this trip to Tokyo Hart was accompanied by Louis Frenkel, who subsequently sent a report back to the company members in London.

Referring to the earlier paper 'How a Voice Gave Me a Conscience' that 'described how a therapeutic community had grown spontaneously around me as a result of my study and use of my voice' (Roy Hart 1967), Hart introduced the notion of 'Objective Voice' through a quotation from Heinz Joachim. (Writing for *Die Welt* on 20 October 1969, Joachim had reviewed *Eight Songs for a Mad King* by Peter Maxwell Davies.)

> 'All this was (banal as the formulation may sound) simply phenomenal, unique, sensational. *Yet it lay beyond all "sensation"*. It was so deeply *stamped*

> *by immediate experience*, it was the art of presentation which, *at every minute, used the means available in a conscious way*, and yet never transgressed *the borderline* that leads to trash ... No other artist could probably realise this part so penetratingly'.
>
> (Roy Hart 'The Objective Voice' 1972 – Hart's original emphasis)

Hart felt that in some way Joachim has understood not only the musical, artistic value of his voice but also the deep integrity and personal stature that underlay his vocal skills:

> It is not likely that there is another artist, who uses his voice in this kind of musical context, who has also devoted 25 years to an intensive study of the psychological implications of the human voice, and to stretching its potential for non-egotistical ends. It is my attitude to my art that is more revolutionary than the particular sounds that fellow artists find they can copy or embellish, I believe the artist should reveal 'the struggle', should show that 'borderline' just beyond what is easily within his powers of expression, and should show himself 'conscious at every minute' of the imperfections and perfections of his total humanity.
>
> (Roy Hart 'The Objective Voice' 1972).

Perhaps the key word here for understanding what Hart means by 'The Objective Voice' is 'non-egotistical' (Roy Hart 'The Objective Voice' 1972).

Hart then refers to another review, this time of *Beschreibungen der Inneren Erfahrungen*, composed for his voice and five instruments by Meinhart Rudenauer and commissioned by the Austrian Radio, that had recently been performed in Vienna: 'the human voice (baritone solo) is exposed to an extraordinary test of endurance, which Roy Hart, an English singer, dedicatedly and unegotistically accomplished' (Engweth 1972). For Hart, this reviewer's response 'reveals that the purpose of my work is slowly seeping through to the compartmentalised Western mind' (Roy Hart 'The Objective Voice' 1972) and he went on to touch on schizophrenia, a theme that he often reiterated in other contexts. Here, Hart was speaking to a reappraisal of schizophrenia at that time through works such as R.D Laing and Aaron Esterson's *Sanity, Madness and the Family* (1964) or Mary Barnes and Joseph Berk's *Two Accounts of a Journey Through Madness* (1971). Theatrically, Hart may have been inspired, as were many of his peers, by the post-war innovations of theatre theorist and director **Antonin Artaud**, which were fuelled by Artaud's own mental health struggles.

> **Antonin Artaud** (1896–1948) was a theatre theorist, playwright and director whose writings have had a profound influence on many major theatre artists from the mid-twentieth century to today. His writings and practice invoked a visceral, immersive style of theatre as a challenge to the dominance of realism. He wanted to shake audiences loose from what he perceived as their complacency and he used movement and embodiment in performance to achieve a heightened audience response. He looked to ritual and blood sacrifice as images to embody a 'Theatre of Cruelty' – and was influenced by diverse theatrical forms such as Greek theatre and Balinese dance. Artaud struggled with mental health issues and addiction and spent time in institutions. His writings include *The Theatre of Cruelty* (1933), *The Theatre and its Double* (1938) and the play *The Cenci* (1935).

In 'The Objective Voice' Hart articulates why he has concentrated so much on the voice as a bridge between body and mind, between the conscious and unconscious. Accordingly, Hart strove to educate his voice:

> to produce at will a great variety of timbres and nuances that relate to immediate experience rather than to a clever, intellectually acted simulation of experience, I had to gain in my body the knowledge of my comprehensive humanity.
> (Roy Hart 'The Objective Voice' 1972)

He then describes the work on the voice in the studio with his students:

> They attack with the utmost effort of body and will the different centres of energy – a form of shock treatment for the cells, a biological shake that one hopes will occasionally spark off a new communication between two yearning synapses. Certain sounds stimulate the cortex, others vibrate the genitals, almost all are controlled by the diaphragm and the mind, and the most rewarding sounds involve a fine, tight-rope-walking communication between head, guts, diaphragm, finger-tips and toes.
> (Roy Hart 'The Objective Voice' 1972)

For Hart, stretching the human voice alone was not sufficient. It had to be an all-inclusive approach that included stretching one's self awareness and awareness of others. The personal psychological dimension and social development were essential elements to what he called the Objective Voice. He enumerates a long list of activities that comprise this approach to building awareness, including working in the community, rehearsals, performing cabarets, tracking dreams, analysing relationships, and a broader study of people, books and articles.

He recognises, however, that such a demanding programme of study and dedication is not necessarily suited to everyone. Clearly, certain individuals, already gifted, may find such a context beneficial and therapeutic, but it can also work well for those 'who have patience, humility, courage and above all a desire to grow'. He warns though that: 'It is NOT suitable for those whose body chemistry has been so far influenced by traumatic experiences or stubborn death wish so that the Will for Action has been warped beyond repair' (Roy Hart 'The Objective Voice' 1972). Above all, he acknowledges that 'It takes respect for change and stability and a great generosity of spirit to be able to stay in my theatre community for any length of time, but I have watched people who were trapped in a one-octave way of living growing towards the eight-octave life in disciplined freedom' (Roy Hart 'The Objective Voice' 1972).

Summing up the kind of music therapy he practices Hart writes:

> It must now be clear that the music therapy I practise is highly active [...] in our context even our listening takes an active form registering where the sounds come from in the body, and with what differing dynamics they are produced in different individuals; registering the known personality of the person making the sounds and the context in which he or she is making them (i.e. mindful of that person's dreams, daily actions over the years, relationships and so on). The sounds which I make vocally have a background of maximum thought, maximum sensitivity to others, maximum personal feeling and involvement, and maximum self-discipline.
>
> (Roy Hart 'The Objective Voice' 1972).

This attention to the 'wider picture', to the whole mindset and, one might say, to the ethos behind Hart's approach is what can be understood by 'The Objective Voice'. From one point of view, it is an almost utopic, altruistic conception of the artist/singer: one who is not blinded by their own creative force, but rooted in a deep comprehension of their own responsibility to oneself and others. Hart would sometimes refer to 'pig artists' as being the type of artists who might ride roughshod over others, thus not only destroying the well-being of those around but also putting into danger their own capacity to look into their own shadows and unresolved lacunae. Such a programme of study as he extolled was designed to reduce the 'ego' and increase a sensitivity to one's own many-sidedness, and the complex ground of personal relationships. The 'singing' work, by its insistence on going to one's very extremes, in a sense, to the end of oneself, forced the 'singer' into confrontation with their worst fears, but also, paved the ground for revealing new facets of oneself. It was a 'breaking down' and a 'restructuring', using the voice as the primordial tool, the filter for that process. Hart also referred to this, using metaphors borrowed from *The Bacchae*, as 'dismemberment' and subsequent 'redemption' or 'rebirth'. Thus the 'old ego' died in order for a fuller human being to emerge. This theme is the background to his work, both artistically and therapeutically, and it informs the performances realised in his lifetime and gives us an insight into how he conducted his personal and professional relationships. Looked at from the outside, his almost rigid insistence on 'integrity' and being true to his ethical aspirations may seem like an exaggerated stance, that led to him breaking relations with three major composers, when he certainly had a very successful career before him (as detailed in **Chapter One**).

Company member Louis Frenkel who had, as mentioned, accompanied Hart on this trip to Japan, wrote at length two weeks later about their trip and their interactions with the congress participants and Japanese culture. He described the moment when Roy Hart was to deliver his lecture:

> At the time that Roy was called to deliver his lecture, he dispensed with the prepared text and played the tape of *Eight Songs for a Mad King* which as I listened struck me as being a brilliant improvisation and utterly germane to the atmospheric conditions.
>
> (Frenkel 1972)

Clearly Roy Hart, true to his own maxim of living in the moment, had discarded his written text for an apparently more provocative action: playing the tape of this work which featured his extraordinary vocal play and an evocation of madness in the form of George III. This sparked off a variety of different reactions and, in a sense, enabled him to articulate his own stance in an immediate and uncompromising way.

NOTES ON *BIODRAME*

Although Hart made scant reference in his writings to his own personal journey as an actor, or his views on acting, he did leave a powerful testimony through his annotated text of *Biodrame*, a dramatic poem that Serge Béhar had written for him in 1972. (This essay and annotated text, '*Biodrame*....is somewhat the story of my life', is also referenced closely in **Chapter Three**.) Hart wrote these notes beside each stanza and they formed part of a letter to an unnamed French television producer, in which Hart clarified and asserted his particular philosophy and how it affected his personal and artistic activities, and their social and political impact. In his letter to the TV producer on 31 August 1973 Hart sums up what he understands to be the main theme of *Biodrame*:

> Most so-called avant-garde theatres, operas, etc. are beginning to recognize the intrinsic significance of what is called the cry: they no longer hear it as mere noise, but as having its own philosophical implications, not only for the evolution of musical theatre, but for people who sing, play, speak, that is to say for the human race. It is therefore necessary that your program should take into full account the way in which RHT, as related to the late Alfred Wolfsohn, has come out of the cry to reinstate the word. We have not outgrown the cry, which we have been practising for over twenty-five years, but on the contrary, we have absorbed it into every fibre of our being. For us, therefore, the word, i.e. philosophy, must remain paramount.
> (Roy Hart '*Biodrame*....is somewhat the story of my life' 1973)

Wolfsohn's influence on Hart can be seen in his analysis of Béhar's work, and relationship between biology and the voice:

> Through the use of the word, and its relevance to the voice and to the entire biological framework and mindscape which make up the individual, Serge Béhar, being a Doctor, poet and philosopher, wrote *Biodrame* in which he has expressed in theatrical terms the central thesis of that which led us to study the cry. The cry as expressed by dying soldiers, babies, human beings in distress, and also manifest in outbursts of *joie de vivre*. This means that man, as an individual, is the root of society. ... I do not present *Biodrame* as a straightforward poem, but this solo literally expresses vocally, through a longstanding organic process of integration, the relationship between body control and vocal control, in other words self-control.
> (Roy Hart '*Biodrame*....is somewhat the story of my life' 1973)

In Hart's annotated script of *Biodrame,* the French words in italics refer to the text:

> This is my first singing lesson. Farts, belches etc. are not irrelevant noises, but sounds which belong to the human orchestra. *'Le sang clair'* (the clear sound) is a tenor sound – generally associated with spirit, light, romantic love, femininity. In *'la rengaine'* (corny song), the traditional concepts of opera, deep voice means body, depth, masculinity. In Roy Hart Theatre both men and women push their voices beyond bass and soprano in search of the human voice, as opposed to the specialised voice.
> (Roy Hart '*Biodrame*….is somewhat the story of my life' 1973)

Hart's distinction between the 'human' voice and the 'specialised' voice, identified here in his notes on the script, is central to his philosophy, and his teachings, and can be traced back to Wolfsohn's taking dark inspiration from the cries of soldiers' desperation in the trenches of World War I. In this annotated script, Hart also writes about a layered, or 'corded sound' that the company experimented with in training, and in performance:

> I represent *'les cordes'* (the chords) with a multiple sound containing several notes in a chord – we call it chorded sound. This sound fascinates many people, for they think this is one of the only sounds they can't imitate. I have often been labelled a vocal phenomenon—not to say a monstrous freak that could attract crowds to a circus […]. Paradoxically, my vocal range of about eight octaves now seems less sensational, *'sans emphase'* (without emphasis), because the sounds I sing without a mask contain all the other sounds and notes I have embodied and filled with meaning during this endless search of pioneer in the desert.
> (Roy Hart '*Biodrame*….is somewhat the story of my life' 1973).

Corded sound with its multiple strands can evoke a world that seems not quite human, alien even, and as such is striking when used effectively in performance: developing the sound fully justifies Hart's insistence on including all the potential of the human voice. Hart also details the link he perceives between personal transformation and its effect on the body politic, when speaking about the value of human relationships:

> It is therefore necessary for the 'I' to make contact with the 'thou'. The human relationship of two people, not in competition, but in co-operation – that is,

> the couple in the most sacred sense of the word – is the basis of relationships
> with others, actors then audience. In the Roy Hart Theatre we give a great
> importance to human dialogue – in private, when for instance friends have tea
> together in the club restaurant, and in public, in the meetings, the whole group
> regularly attends – because it is a source of creative substance for our perfor-
> mances which in turn make our so-called private life richer.
>
> (Roy Hart '*Biodrame*....is somewhat the story of my life' 1973)

THE INTERVIEWS

Several interviews Roy Hart gave afford us an insight into his views and his own perception of his work and its relevance – his detractors sometimes criticised him as being unnecessarily elusive or mercurial, but Hart would have maintained that was a stance he needed to take to protect his work. These extracts and writings, many sourced at the Roy Hart Theatre Archive, offer a contemporaneous glimpse into the workings of a large artistic collective under the leadership of a central, contentious but charismatic figure.

PRIMER ACTO

As mentioned earlier, perhaps the most significant of these interviews was a series of meetings organised by *Primer Acto*, Spain's foremost theatre magazine in March 1971 during a season of workshops that Hart directed at the *Escuela Superior de Arte Dramático* of Madrid. The interviews were conducted by José Monleón, Pepe Estruch and Ricardo Domenech. We have included substantial extracts of this interview below in a bid to capture Hart's critical voice and some of the theories underpinning his work. The first part of the interviews covers Hart's early life, his meeting Wolfsohn and the beginnings of his path as a pioneer in voice. Hart then spoke about his company:

> What else can I say? I never basically intended to create what is now called the Roy Hart Theatre. The Roy Hart Theatre was created because of a collective interest in what we now call the Human Voice, in contrast to what is called the specialised voice – that is to say: bass, baritone, soprano, etc. In embodying these ideas, men and women of all ages, of all professions, have united – and have united for the pursuit of an idea that is much greater than me, myself or

the self in each one of us. They have stayed with me because they want to continue in this idea – but I did not set out to form a group as such.

(Monleón, Estruch and Domenech 1971)

Hart spoke to the care with which the company treated every aspect of performance, and a perception that this led some critics to conclude that the work was overly planned or choreographed:

> Some observers judge us too 'serious' because we do not let one intonation, one gesture pass unprepared. This could become irritating, but it leads us to a care-full-ness: to enunciation, to discrimination, to good models, to interest for the fellow-actor. The question of 'carefulness' initially referred to the question 'who am I?' and has inevitably forced me to become knowledgeable about these people, these individuals that enter into my orbit, in such a way that it is absolutely impossible for me to think in abstract terms.

(Monleón, Estruch and Domenech 1971)

During their conversation Monleón and Domenech try to engage Hart with specific questions related to the actor and his approach to actor-training, but Hart tends to answer tangentially, often returning to philosophical or ethical reflections. He asserts that the driving force behind his work is the notion that: 'I am greater than myself'. Hart contrasts the flash of inspiration and artistic enlightenment that might issue forth during one of his lessons, with the need for the student to integrate this into an ongoing growth process, where routine and the daily challenges of life act as a counterbalance. Only in this way can the artist avoid the traps of exuberant egomania or deflated pessimism, and achieve a sense of proportion.

Speaking about the role of the spectator, Hart refutes the notion of voyeurism and prefers to invite the spectator to take part in the performance as revelation or illumination. Only after the performance can they engage actively with his work through the channels he proposes: private lessons, group sessions and eventually inclusion in rehearsals and performance. However, he does open up the possibility, exceptionally, of an audience member being included consciously in a live performance. But he warns:

> I do not believe in hypnotic participation. Instead, afterwards they can talk with me, with the aim of not merely participating in a 'happening', but rather of wanting to enter into a long path of self-studies that will finally take them to acting.

(Monleón, Estruch and Domenech 1971)

Theatre for Hart was never a light or dilettante form of expression. It required dedication and long-term commitment and implied loyalty to the work itself and to those with whom it was practised. In this sense Hart believed in honour: honouring the philosophical and psychological principles that underpinned his work, and that he defined in a number of principles and metaphors: 'The voice is the muscle of the soul', 'The moment of greatest peril coincides with the moment of greatest hope', 'synthesis of opposites', 'height based on depth', 'it's the mysterious organisation of minute matter' (Monleón, Estruch and Domenech 1971). He subscribed to the teachings of Martin Buber, a Viennese Jew whose central thesis was what he called the I/Thou relationship that restored value to the nature of human relationships and endowed them with an artistic and spiritual dimension (Buber 1923). For example, in interview, company member Enrique Pardo spoke to Hart's philosophy as influenced by his Jewish background, and how it placed Hart in a position to be Pardo's 'ethical mentor':

> I call him today an ethical genius – that is why I bring in aspects like his Jewish background and his relationship to Talmudic studies. […] I was more interested in having an ethical mentor – someone who could think in terms of deep ethical perspectives and ethical behaviour, in life […] A guru is an important notion in Vedic traditions [for] a master teacher who preaches what he does, and does what he preaches, and that was one of the things that Roy Hart would put forward.
>
> (Pardo 2019)

When asked if he had observed different stages in the development of the company, Hart was clear that the company had gone through several phases of growth, always intimately connected with opening new vocal territory amongst its members. This might be in the form of an individual breakthrough – a member of the company who had never sung high sounds might find that this area opens up revealing a rich mine of hitherto hidden vocal potential – another might dig up a cavernous roar that sent shivers down the spine – or it might be an ensemble improvisation that pushed back the boundaries of what seemed possible for a chorus of human voices. These moments of enlightenment were always immediately filtered through discussion, observation and reflection so they became assimilated into the very fabric of the company and could be recalled and, in some cases, integrated later into production. Each new vocal discovery was mirrored by an intense exploration of what this discovery meant for Hart and his collaborators on both a personal and social level.

Finally, for Hart voice was not a function of anatomy, be it larynx, diaphragm or lungs, but a dynamic reflection of the personality. He concluded the interview by commenting on his relationship to words:

> To begin with, every pioneer has to take an extreme position. Mine was interpreted as an attack against the word, which is absurd: it is precisely my love for the word and the consideration of how the word has been abused, which made me ask the question: 'What originated the word?' I want the word to be born again.
>
> (Monleón, Estruch and Domenech 1971)

Given the dearth of writings describing his studio methodology by Roy Hart himself, we also include the following from his Interview with Peter Haley-Dunne. In late December 1969 Haley-Dunne, a young writer and journalist, began to frequent Hart's meetings and rehearsals. At Hart's request, he interviewed him. The following extract reveals how Hart perceived his dual role as therapist and creative agent. It also crystallises his basic belief that excellence can come from the humblest origins: a society based not on blunt superiority but on a subtler form of merit. In meetings he would refer to these notions in an almost biblical terms: 'The first shall be last' and 'Something will come out of nothing' were sayings he would use to draw the company's attention to principles that underlay both his own choices and spontaneous occurrences within the company. In this unpublished interview, Hart revisits what he means by theatre:

> Total theatre – the religious nature of theatre as a binding force [...] I rather see psychotherapy as a method of investigating what binds a group or family together – one is attempting to raise the factors which make a relationship inherently possible to the level of an art, by looking at it with insight rather than as some act of God, devil or grace. I don't believe in grace. I believe in hard work and effort. I call my group my 'synthetic family' and I like to juxtapose the relationship between that and the biological family [...] I say that blood is not thicker than water: water is the stuff of life – the stuff of life is therapy, which ultimately leads to creativity, art and theatre.
>
> (Haley-Dunne 1969)

Here, Hart goes on to assert his standpoint when it comes to evaluating criticisms of 'amateurism' in some of the members of the company:

> I believe in a meritocracy based on absolute mediocrity. By that I mean that the kingdom of art is within. Establish that first: then start work. In contrast to other theatre people, I don't audition. I set out to discover who I was, not to lobby votes for people. The fact that you were fighting for an idea was the first step: it initially attracted mediocrities and all the outcasts of society, but because we fight together, we have established a cohesiveness based on time and effort. Anyone who wants to stop running and start working will reach this kingdom, but this automatically weeds out those who don't want to stop running.
>
> (Haley-Dunne 1969)

This notion of mediocrity is very much at odds, though, with Hart's own professional career, where his virtuosity was rewarded. Hart says something very interesting about singing on pitch here, and the aesthetics of professional vocal performance:

> We all sing out of tune basically – if we haven't the humility to realise that we will go around saying: 'Get out, you are not a professional – be an audience'. The person who sings out of tune can teach the person who sings in tune a lesson – humility.
>
> (Haley-Dunne 1969)

This points to a tension or paradox at the centre of Hart's training — which aims to work with the voice of the performer as it is, requiring humility, but also works to develop vocal quality, which implies an inherent need for change.

THE WRITINGS OF DOROTHY HART

In reviewing Roy Hart's writings and interviews, we need to take into account the considerable contribution offered by other members of the company, particularly Dorothy Hart. Dorothy played a central part in articulating Roy Hart's approach to theatre and life through a series of lengthy notes that she wrote for production programmes (playbills). These form a chain, linking *The Bacchae* from the company's debut in 1969, to *L'Economiste* the last play the company produced before Roy Hart's death in May 1975. (We include substantial quotation from Dorothy's writing in this section as much of the studio practice and work-in-progress was documented in her writings, more so than in writings by Roy Hart.)

Linda Wise, Dorothy Hart's niece and founder member of the company, has commented on Dorothy's unique role in Roy Hart's emergence as a leader and pioneer. Here, Wise makes an uncompromising statement in relation to the origins of Roy Hart's writings. While it is not possible to prove this outright based on the available archival evidence, there is plenty of anecdotal evidence to support the view that Dorothy was central to Roy Hart's artistic achievements and critical output:

> I discovered that it is most likely that she [Dorothy Hart] was the author of many of the papers and certainly even if the ideas were Roy's, she was the person to whom he would he turn for the editing, clarifying, re-writing etc.
>
> (Wise 2021)

Here Wise reiterates her assertion made earlier in interview: 'Almost everything he wrote was written by Dorothy – because he didn't write, Roy, ... she was an academic, you know, so you could see the intelligence (Wise 2019). And her argument is supported by Paul Silber who has written on his own Roy Hart website: 'There was virtually nothing that Roy signed as having been written by him that actually had not first been worked on by Dorothy' (Silber 'Who was Dorothy Hart?' n.d.).

Wise describes her aunt as an extraordinarily talented actor, pianist and flamenco dancer, 'Whatever she did on stage was usually stunning', and mused in interview on how

> it would be interesting to see how much she influenced [Hart's] thinking. I think she put a lot into the writing and rewriting of the text [of *L'Economiste*] but I wasn't always present during their writing phase. [...] She had a humanity about her, [...] she was about the only person who dared to counter him, a lot people were able to cope with the situation [in rehearsal] because of her presence. She coached him in *Eight Songs for a Mad King* – without Dorothy he would never have been able to sing that role.
>
> (Wise 2019)

In interview and elsewhere, Wise has noted that Dorothy's role was in actuality a difficult thing to define given how easy it is to presume that Dorothy's role as wife created a supporting role for her within the company:

> Her role was not only precious – it was essential as the community developed around Roy Hart. And in retrospect I feel that she must have really challenged

him on deeply ethical issues. Dorothy also merits recognition as the exceptional person and artist she became. I really feel her life was her art. She lived her life crossing boundaries, questioning norms. Never would I call her the woman behind or even beside Roy Hart – her spirit was too free for such a position, her mind too fine and her inner life too rich. She accompanied Roy Hart as his legal wife and precious companion.

(Wise 2014)

Wise remembered Dorothy having 'individual work [sessions] with the actor's role' (Wise 2019), and Dorothy Hart also directed the full company as co-director for *The Singer and The Song* (1971) and *and* (1972).

Dorothy Hart's programme note for *The Bacchae* entitled 'God is dead. Long live …?' outlines the philosophical or even ideological background to the company's version of the play:

Euripides' *The Bacchae* has been chosen to express our philosophy of Abraxas and the Rope (Abraxas = the creative synthesis of opposites: the rope is a symbol of our method of achieving and containing Abraxas) … It is obvious that Euripides himself was aware of the stark reality of psychological laws and how they worked, and though he may at times appear to cast his gods in a poor light, the danger of belittling their power, the power of unconscious drives, is constantly and compellingly reiterated. The workings of psychological laws are as real and ruthless today as they ever were, whilst the dangers of unaware behaviour and blind projection are more terrifying than in Euripides' day because the rope of religion, the idea of a hierarchy, political or otherwise, have been cast aside and replaced by nothing, and larger masses of people are losing an awareness of any need to have a rope to contain their multi-dimensional natures. A warning shout is urgently needed NOW … The story of Pentheus is seen in psychological terms: the disintegration of his persona follows a pattern typical of mental breakdown: the ego is killed for the sake of further development.

(Dorothy Hart 'God is dead. Long live …?' 1969)

Dorothy Hart goes on to describe how this approach to *The Bacchae* is rendered in the company's version:

One of the many methods used in this play is to be seen in the constant interplay between the upright position of Homo Sapiens and the supine position experienced by his progenitors, between an infinite variety of mass touch and the experience of individual separation. There are several instances of 'heaps on the floor'— first the amoebic mass at the beginning of the play. Here we imagine the physical feel of the amoebic and the effort required to pull out a separate individuated existence, and this imagining is given a chance of embodiment by simulating in our own bodies something of the nature of that amoebic experience. A later heap is the heap of snakes: each body can experience the feeling of friction as it seeks to move out of the 'sea' onto dry land, and a sensation of the desperate need for legs ... other instances of constant awareness of touch in finger, elbow, backbone or toe occur throughout the play linked to different emotions, the hard touch of aggression (the Kali scene or the carrying of Pentheus) the huddling touch of insecurity (the descending into hell described by T:S: Eliot's *The Hollow Men*) and so on.

(Dorothy Hart 'God is dead. Long live ...?' 1969)

Later she clarifies the attitude of the actors towards the production and how it too had a ritual meaning and purpose for those performing, and was an integral part of their approach to training:

We attempt during every performance to 'die' to that self which takes the Present for granted as likely to carry out our preconceptions for us. We do not make changes and confusion for the sake of shocking each other and the audience for some masochistic purpose, but for the sake of keeping ourselves open to the growth process, for being prepared for the unexpected.

(Dorothy Hart 'God is dead. Long live ...?' 1969)

Speaking about Roy Hart's role, Dorothy says:

Roy Hart has been the main producer, inspired leader and task-master, but rehearsals have as often been led and the production vastly influenced by others, Robert Harvey in particular. [...] Roy Hart usually confines himself to conducting and leading the background orchestration, but he is as likely to enter in on the action of the play in some other role as any member of the cast is likely to put forward a suggestion which will alter the tenor of the whole production.

(Dorothy Hart 'God is dead. Long live ...?' 1969)

Dorothy Hart underlines the fact that the use of a wide range of sounds, both beautiful and ugly, in speech and song, is not an arbitrary one, in this useful insight into the company's rehearsal process. She defends the fact that both male and female performers use ranges that challenge conventional preconceptions of the male or female voice:

> Both male and female performers interchange with 'male' and 'female' sounds, and this is our rebellion—the long-haired men, the male-voiced masculine women are outward expressions of what is fundamentally an inner problem—the search for the hermaphroditic personality in each one of us.
>
> (Dorothy Hart 'God is dead. Long live ...?' 1969)

Interestingly, Linda Wise remembered the company's working against formal training and an overemphasis on aesthetics in professional performance as having a key impact on the work of the company and the voices of its members: 'There was a total resistance [to beauty in singing] by some members and I think it was because they had to fight so much against this one way of training the voice that it went in the opposite way' (Wise 2019). Wise recalled training later in life in *bel canto* (an Italian opera singing style with an emphasis on technique) to recover some of that beauty in her own voice.

Dorothy Hart's programme note for *The Bacchae* notes the centrality of dreams in the work of the company, and expands on how the members of the cast were encouraged to engage with the play by bringing their own associations in the form of dream images, key words, songs and poems, whilst also framing the play in a host of quotes from topical articles in the press that touched on the themes of *The Bacchae* from a variety of viewpoints:

> Rehearsals entered a very personal phase where someone's significant dream was recalled, some personality clash during the day was referred to and possibly re-enacted, someone's aura or facial expression stopped the action of the play and a spontaneous by-play was grafted onto the theme, and all of this by the genus of dream logic.
>
> (Dorothy Hart 'God is dead. Long live ...?' 1969)

The inclusion of dreams as a starting point and spur to collective creativity is a recurring theme in Dorothy Hart's introduction. From her we learn that: 'The cast's philosophy embraces a continual study of each and everyone's dreamlife, and this is always related to the waking situation'. Dreams present their images in sometimes apparently illogical sequence. Events take place in dreams that are 'impossible', but they make sense in the dreams' logic and context. This parallel logic of dreams, its gift for bending reflection, and representing reality in a quirky way inspired the company's approach to the play. It allowed it to introduce many unscripted events and material into the fabric of the play, much in the manner that a dream, magpie-like, dips into a Pandora's box of images, to unravel its own logic:

> The dream world makes great use of fusion, metamorphosis and doubling-up of characters -mixtures of male and female, animal, vegetable and mineral. This characteristic has come about also quite spontaneously with our production, because we started from the premise, as a dream does, of bringing out the psychological meaning for us.
>
> (Dorothy Hart 'God is dead. Long live ...?' 1969)

Eventually a performer was assigned to particularly embody this dream aspect in the production, and it was Dorothy Hart herself, who explained: 'out of this philosophy the concept of a "dreamer" for our production was evolved. A particular performer was chosen to represent the bias of the dreamer and her role was to "stamp" her personal associations or interpretations—on the action of the play' (Dorothy Hart 'God is dead. Long live ...?' 1969). Although, eventually, some of her interventions were set, the actual words and timing were not, there was always a measure of improvisation.

Dorothy Hart sums up by speaking to the company's politics during this period of unrest throughout mainland Europe, the US and elsewhere, as evidenced by violent student riots and demonstrations in 1968 against the Vietnam War, against communist restrictions of freedoms and for workers' rights:

> We do not take part in student riots or take an active role in politics in general, but we are forming policies that foretell the coming social structure. The Greeks put on masks: we are taking them off, and showing who we are.
>
> (Dorothy Hart 'God is dead. Long live ...?' 1969)

Later in 1969, for Roy Hart Theatre's revised version of *The Bacchae* entitled *The Bacchae presented as The Frontae*, Dorothy wrote about the inclusion of musical instruments influenced by Roy Hart's ongoing collaborations with contemporary composers:

> Tonight's performance will be the first in which musical and other instruments are used, as an extension of the body's ability to express itself. This came about in response to Roy Hart's recent contact with three well-known composers of our time, Henze, Maxwell-Davies, Stockhausen, and their starkly different

approaches to instruments and instrumentalists with whom they work. Being very aware of this moment in history as it reveals itself in our personal lives, modern music and art, politics, science and the whole spectrum of human projections, Roy Hart knew there was a general historical evolutionary reason why composers at opposite ends of the experimental musical pole such as Henze and Stockhausen had both made an immediate strong response to their first hearing of the sounds in his voice.

(Dorothy Hart notes on the production 1969)

As part of a recording of a rehearsal for *and* performed 1972 to 1973, Dorothy described her own personal process for a scene called 'The Singing Lesson'. This recording gives us insight into the nature of the 'singing lesson' as Dorothy defines it here. It reflects very closely how Hart and the company used the metaphor of the singing lesson to represent a life and work ethic:

Usually at this point in the performance, I rediscover myself in sound, I sing. I give myself what we call a singing lesson. I discover my body, singing. Tonight, the spirit has dictated otherwise. Singing, in the Roy Hart Theatre, is a special word which carries 47 years of accrued meaning. It includes what I'm doing now, speaking, with words (Dorothy Hart a rehearsal note for *and* 1972).

In the recording Dorothy Hart likens this way of singing to meditation or prayer, and described her daily practice. She also spoke to the power of language, word choice and the connection of language to the body:

It is a form of prayer, summoning the whole body, not only on Sundays or maybe 10 minutes to an hour each day, but if possible, every minute, every second. Summoning the body to concentrate on evaluating, on making balanced values. This is singing. To be true to myself tonight I need to speak with words. We live in a verbal world. I am a verbal person by inclination, or I have become more so. These words we use, the way in which we speak them, with differing intensities of bodily involvement. Honesty. The way we use words really concerns me, us. Last night I lay awake for many hours wrestling to embody in my own experience the meaning of certain words, so common, yet so individual. They contain peace and dynamite, diffidence and passion. I would like you to share with me tonight while I sing, or pray, concentrating on these few powerful words. Singing or prayer intention, I love you, living art, husband, wife, lover ...
(Dorothy Hart a rehearsal note for *and* 1972)

In March 1975 Dorothy Hart wrote a personal essay and analysis entitled *L'Economist: A Dream of Reality* – *L'Economiste* being the play that the company were preparing at that point for a tour in Austria and Spain. In this substantial document she surveys the whole play, analysing the characters, their relations and actions and how they symbolise the struggles and resolution that the play enacts. Her essay, complemented by articles by Vivienne Young, Lucienne Deschamps, Boris Moore and Robert Harvey, constituted a 23-page programme note translated into French and German. Overall, the programme note recounts the story behind the creation of *L'Economiste*, letter exchanges between Hart and Serge Béhar, the author, and the rewriting process, as well as the musical and choreographic approach:

> This play is about Human nature, as the actors of Roy Hart Theatre perceive it. One can appreciate it quite simply as a dream, an impressionist painting, a ballet or a musical: but for those who prefer to dig deeper into its meaning, further analysis of the play proves fruitful.
>
> (Dorothy Hart 1975)

Dorothy Hart provides a detailed overview of the play in this programme note (this play and its production are described more fully in **Chapter Three**). Dorothy inserts herself here between Hart and the playwright, to give the audience a point of access to the play and its significance to the company. It's hard not to read some of the personalities of the company into this description of characters, especially given how the play evolved through the company's redrafting of Béhar's text, and how the company was evolving at this point in its history:

> This play shows how Maurice and Flora slowly and painfully come to that point, moving in a mindscape where 'dream' and 'reality' have significantly undefined boundaries. Flora represents a priceless human quality, possessed by only a few people i.e. that basic intelligence, generosity and courage that makes a human being educable, transformable—Maurice represents the intuitive artist in Man, who in his early fumbling towards wisdom is usually regarded by his fellows as a misfit or a fool—The Customers are the average man and woman, mostly unaware and emotionally unstable—The Masked Men represent the unconscious forces that can possess the bodies of such average men and women, compelling them to hysteria or vindictive mass action—The Family and Worldly Friends are almost self-evident as

> examples of the stifling, life-denying values that can cramp a human being's natural psychic development—Justine is a manifestation of psychic balance—She is the female counterpart of Maurice approaching wisdom along a different road from his—The Technarch's significance may at first seem crudely obvious. He represents the current obsession with technology, and the distorted mechanical figure that hangs on his every word with 'gaga' admiration is a caricature of the kind of 'anima' figure such a man generally finds for himself.
>
> (Dorothy Hart 1975)

Dorothy describes the symbolic weight of the characters, and through this programme note gives the audience a way to connect the play and its contents to the company's director, Hart:

> All of the characters are an aspect of Maurice, conscious man, all are a manifestation of his dream, Roy Hart's dream. For Roy Hart knows that every member of the theatre that has grown around him, his personal search for his total identity through exploring his voice—every member of that theatre is a precious aspect of himself.
>
> (Dorothy Hart 1975)

ROY HART'S LETTERS

Roy Hart maintained a steady stream of letters to his contemporaries, be they from the theatrical, musical or scientific sphere. He wrote to a wide cross-section of people from fields as diverse as psychodrama and architecture, biology and literary criticism. On the whole these were mainly letters presenting his and the company's work and, as often as not, inviting the recipient to see a rehearsal or performance. He exchanged a series of letters with James Roose-Evans, an influential critic, writer and theatre director, who founded the Hampstead Theatre Club. We quote here from one of these letters, written shortly after the company's tour in Spain in October 1971, as it seems to contain the kernel of Hart's approach to theatre, especially in the early days of the company. Unusually for him, he does confide in Roose-Evans, revealing some of his own perceptions about how he and the company present themselves (again, we quote this at length here given the dearth of critical writings on practice and process by Roy Hart). Hart credits Spain for its 'feeling' response to the work, referring perhaps to its extremely diverse cultural history and the reaction to a fascist régime in place at that time under General Franco.

> As you say, Europe does respond more immediately to my work than England, and for obvious historical and psychological reasons Spain responds with the most feeling. […] but not without intelligent insight. […] Our performance in the Teatro Zarzuela in Madrid was received with tremendous applause, […] Yet the nature of Spain's welcome to my work is only in keeping with what she requires of me, and is not much more objective than England's non-understanding of what I was about at The Round House. What I presented at The Round House would have been intuited as intelligible and valuable by the Spanish, because what you saw and found too private and alienating is exactly what they want. You say you saw an affirmation by a community of people of their sensitivity and awareness of one another. At that time, for England especially, that was precisely all I wanted to present to right a balance in certain attitudes towards theatre in this country. *The Bacchae*, as performed by my company at Nancy, had by the time of The Round House, been torn into almost unrecognizable shreds and my company was exposed to the precarious adventure of individual spontaneous sensitizing with each other, some of the cast having only been with us for a matter of weeks.
> (Roy Hart 1971)

Hart details here his perception that the work of the company was more fully understood and appreciated by a mainland European audience than an English one – a perception that, as we know, led to the company's departure from England to southern France in 1974. This urge to relocate to mainland Europe was shared by a number of companies, writers and playwrights, such as English director Peter Brook who moved to Paris in 1971, and English theatre company Footsbarn, which left Cornwall to become an itinerant travelling troupe in 1984, eventually settling in France in 1991. It is not a solely English phenomenon either, Irish playwright Samuel Beckett followed in the footsteps of Irish writer James Joyce when he moved to France, settling in Paris in 1937, and some of America's most famous novelists of what was dubbed 'the lost generation', such as Ernest Hemingway and F. Scott Fitzgerald helped build Paris's reputation as the European centre of culture earlier in the twentieth century. Hart is clearly responding to a charge from Roose-Evans that the work was 'too private and alienating' and defends the work here as necessarily having those qualities – qualities that he believed an English audience was ill-equipped to appreciate:

> It was a stage in our theatrical development, much harder for my company (any company) to perform than what they presented to you the other night. One could even say it was 'unfair' to both cast and audience, but I am not English and anything less 'unfair' would not have been, at that time, a true stepping-stone along the way I have chosen. You observe correctly that my company has matured and certain individuals more than others, but I sense that there is something in the manner in which you compare The Round House and this more recent performance which is misleading.
>
> (Roy Hart 1971)

Hart speaks to his continued commitment to staging a diverse level of theatrical 'talent' as a reflection of the company, and the world at large:

> I am less concerned with the display of skills (that almost inevitably tend to lead to egotistical behaviour and sometimes to stylization) than I am to portray the struggle that a large group of individuals (some far more mature or skilled than others) have, when required to co-operate with each other to find an artistic whole beyond the egotistical. I am interested in containing the inferior, the ugly, imperfect and inadequate alongside the superior, beautiful and polished, within a framework where sufficient individuals know sufficiently what they are about to do this [...]
>
> We stay put and get on with it, the unenviable task of teaching the developed to work with the underdeveloped, not like self-sacrificing Christian missionaries, but like people determined to get the most possible out of life.
>
> Thank you again for your candid and encouraging comments,
> sincerely yours,
> Roy Hart
>
> (Roy Hart 1971)

Hart's opinions on the nature of art and performance were later described in another correspondence, this time in late 1974 with Serge Béhar during exchanges about a play Béhar was to write for Hart and the company. Here Hart stated:

> Twice now you have been ambiguous with yourself and thus with me ... The first time was when you wrote to London saying that you were writing a play for me and us, which would be ready in three months. Three months went by. Nothing. At that time, I asked Lucienne to phone you because I was full of despair. Why despair? It is only now that those who are closest to me are realising that when

> all the forces which made my being into a leader, a father-figure and a psychologist – when all these forces are removed, what can be seen is that which has always been: I AM AN ACTOR THAT IS TO SAY THAT PERFORMANCES ARE MY LIFE-BLOOD.
>
> (Roy Hart 1974)

Hart reveals his ambitions for the human voice in performance as he urges Béhar to write for the company, using strong imagery to appeal to Béhar's artistic sensibilities:

> the voice, dear Serge, must be reinstated, redeemed, reaffirmed [...]. You have a tendency to de-dramatise the nature of art, the nature of dramatic art by presenting it as entertainment rather than a reflection, and a resounding, of the deepest and most precious instrument of the human soul. This is why we perform as we live as we perform—Your play should be about hailing the return of God arm in arm with his friend the Devil. A god who was only on holiday, for a sufficiently long time to fool the revolutionaries that he is dead.
>
> (Roy Hart 1974)

CONVERSATIONS AND PRIVATE LETTERS

> Hour BE LOVED THE AT RE:
>
> Artists have known from time immemorial what Einstein needed to prove scientifically: that matter is the congealed vibration of SOUL. We as ZINGERS employ the only substances that break the SPELL hidden within the wood? the stone? the note? the BODY!! that is HEAT. to allow this matter to reveal its TRUE SHAPE I therefore WARM you; and am warmed by you... .

Roy Hart communicated with his students and later his company through notes, postcards, messages and letters. He developed his ideas and disseminated his work through ongoing conversations with the company as a whole and the individuals within it. A few excerpts from these private conversations have been recorded, although to the authors' knowledge, at the time of writing no recordings were made of his group meetings with the company as a whole. Two letters from the early seventies illustrate how Hart would write to the company using a combination of wordplay, puns and creative spelling to communicate

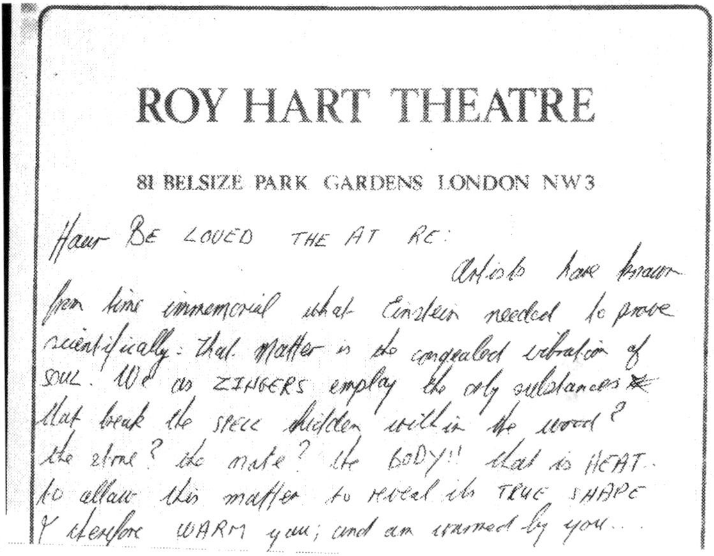

ROY HART THEATRE

81 BELSIZE PARK GARDENS LONDON NW3

Haur Be Loved The At Re:

Artists have known from time immemorial what Einstein needed to prove scientifically: that matter is the congealed vibration of soul. We as ZINGERS employ the only substances that break the space hidden within the word? the stone? the note? the BODY!! that is HEAT. to allow this matter to reveal its TRUE SHAPE & therefore WARM you; and am warmed by you...

Figure 2.1 Personal letter from Roy Hart to the Roy Hart Company (RHT Archive), image courtesy of Ivan Midderigh, RHT Photographic Archives.

his ideas and wishes. The first letter is commented on by Paul Silber by way of explaining Hart's idiosyncratic writing style:

> The origin of 'zingers' was that one of the members of the theatre made a spelling error, but Roy liked it because to use the word 'singers' is, in fact, slightly misleading. Singing for Roy was not a matter of song singing, singing, was for Roy, a code word for life itself.
>
> 'Substances' being, of course, the voice, hence the use of the word 'note' and very importantly 'BODY', since the body is the place where 'HEAT' can be found; 'heat' is a reference to passion. So, by the passion generated by the voice the soul is enabled to emerge in its 'TRUE SHAPE'.
>
> (Paul Silber http://www.roy-hart.com/letter.htm)

A second letter, although addressed to the Roy Hart Theatre as a whole, addresses two members in particular, Saule Ryan and Noah Pikes:

> Dearest Roy Hart Theatre, let it be understood: THE FUTURE belongs to the POET-EDUCAT(H)ER): ATTACK do not let your PASSIONS LIE. I wish SHAULE and Dennis to give a SIR MON on how SEA MEN is EJECTED if it is not to be RE-JECTED, the sound must now move into the WORD ... attack those, whose power suppressed your sound, by giving your words the power that you have mine(d) from the SOUND and INJECT yourself into your law-full HOME.
>
> (Roy Hart 1970)

Writing about Roy Hart and his definition of singing Enrique Pardo asserts:

> His was a philosophy of personal transcendence transmitted through a Socratic style of teaching and developed within the hermetic context of a theatre community. The root metaphor of their approach to the voice was the notion of singing, with as broad a physiological and metaphorical understanding as possible. Involving self-confrontation and self-knowledge through expression, its motto could have been: 'You are, or you become, what you sing.' The singer pits her or himself against the notion of an 'eight octave voice', a concept meant to include the full range of human potential. To speak therefore of 'extended voice range' within this tradition could be said to be an academically correct understatement; Wolfsohn, and certainly Hart, would have spurned such a label as a technical euphemism.
>
> (Pardo 2003)

Two letters written by Hart, the first in 1966 when he was visiting his mother in Israel, and the second later around 1972 when his company was already established at The Abraxas Club, seem to convey both his fervent commitment to his chosen path and his enduring covenant with those he loved. As a man he was unstintingly demanding of himself and often of those closest to him, but this can only be fully appreciated if we bear in mind his genuine and contagious warmth allied to a seemingly infinite patience and attention to detail, which added up to compassionate and insightful loving. From Israel he wrote to his then small circle of students and friends:

> We all long for the absolutely true, the invulnerable, permanent. But since in any given situation we can imagine things as other than they are, and actions must be interpreted – where is the truth in a situation? It must reside in moving the action from a physical – real –manifestation to a meta-physical place – ACTING.

In other words the LOVE I show you is not based on what messages I'm getting from you – only in some cases – otherwise I would cease loving and start being independent, cut off, i.e. hateful. Love in other words, or truth, is our SEARCH FOR IT!! our <u>will</u> for it.

(Roy Hart 1966)

Some years later, during an absence from England, he wrote to the company – which had in the meanwhile more or less doubled in size – as they prepared for an upcoming performance. His closing words were:

On Friday night before you perform let there be SILENCE, an attitude of contemplation […] I will try to put myself in touch with you from 6:30 p.m. <u>PRECISELY</u> ONWARDS until you FEEL that there is attention in the court. DO NOT SPEAK ... contemplate, do NOT try to play dazzling games, have the courage to let your inner voice direct you. All other directors and actors and so-called artists have forgotten that there is a TRADITION of the COSMOS which they deny in favour of being clever or brilliant, in other words everything which denies that life is INNOCENT, HEALING, REPARATIVE, it is at once the saddest and the happiest of all things,
   a SMILE,
   which is what I send THOU,
   THY ROY

(Roy Hart 1970)

3

FOUR PRODUCTIONS BY RHT (1967–76)

THE BACCHAE

By 1966 Hart felt the time had come to challenge his group of actors to a full-length production and expose them and himself to wider public scrutiny. The fury and revels of Dionysus must have inspired him and offered a tempting vehicle for his boundary-breaking vocal work. In addition, the conflict between the conservative Pentheus and the androgynous god Dionysus echoed his own struggles for recognition within what he perceived as repressive cultural norms. Dionysus symbolised for Hart the unchaining of libidinous and creative forces (through, in his case, the medium of the voice) but also the violence that such a liberation can unleash and the tragic cost of denying that these forces exist.

> **The Bacchae,** first performed posthumously in 405 B.C., is arguably Euripedes' most famous tragedy. Euripedes was born around 480 B.C. on the Greek island of Salamis, and died about 406 B.C. *The Bacchae* won first prize at the Athens Dionysia Festival. Based on the myth of the god Dionysus, it tells the story of how the god returns to his native Thebes to claim allegiance from the present

King, Pentheus. Pentheus, however, refuses to acknowledge the god, tries to imprison him and stop the Bacchic rites. These rites, that send the celebrants into ecstatic states, bordering on madness, have already gained many followers including his own mother, Agave. In *The Bacchae*, Dionysus fulfils the role of the protagonist, his goal being to be recognised as a god: he is obstructed by Pentheus the antagonist, who attempts to thwart him. This conflict comes to a head when Pentheus is tricked by a seductive Dionysus into spying on the revels of Agave and the chorus of celebrants, also referred to as maenads. Mistaken for a wild lion, Pentheus is torn to pieces, dismembered by Agave and the crowd, and is thus punished for his blind obstinacy in denying Dionysus his due place as a god. Dionysus' wrath is appeased and he has found the recognition he demanded.

Figure 3.1 Dorothy Hart with the chorus of *The Bacchae* 1969, image courtesy of Ivan Midderigh, RHT Photographic Archives.

In *The Bacchae* Dionysus is depicted in a number of guises. At the beginning of the play he appears as a mortal man, then as 'a fellow with golden hair flowing in scented ringlets' (Vellacott 1954: 188) or an 'effeminate foreigner' (ibid.: 192); later he is described as the bull-horned god, whose head is wreathed with writhing snakes. Dionysus has the gift of transformation, bringing together the human and the animal, the violent and the soft, and his rites may evoke madness as well as ecstasy. Themes of transformation, disguise and gender blurring occur throughout the play, and the company made full use of them, sometimes by cross-gender casting, sometimes by stretching voices to extremes, where the lines between traditionally accepted norms for male and female voices were put under pressure.

What's more *The Bacchae* offered fertile ground for the chorus-style approach Hart had espoused in his studio work. The main role of Dionysus was performed by three actors – Elizabeth Mayer, Marita Günther and Barrie Irwin. They formed an astonishing hydra-headed protagonist. Irwin was closest to the bull nature of Dionysus, Günther the avenging godhead and Mayer the androgynous shape-shifter. Before them stood the extreme masculine inflexibility of Pentheus (Louis Frenkel), who finally succumbs to his repressed sexual curiosity, which proves to be his downfall as he is torn apart by the maenad chorus led by his own mother Agave (Robert Harvey). Throughout this tragedy the chorus is a protean character, sometimes witness, sometimes storyteller, sometimes itself the protagonist, alongside Dionysus, shaping the action. The chorus strophes combine heightened lyricism with violent accelerating chants. It is the collective madness of the maenads, Dionysus' followers, but it is also the oracle of wisdom and balance.

> Kevin Crawford remembers: *The long choric odes are tightly choreographed and the text is sometimes declaimed in unison, sometimes spoken by a single voice, sometimes half-sung. The end of the play, where all actors were still onstage, was contemplative, almost salutary, the Bacchic rite having been expiated, the God revenged, the king reduced to bloody shreds, the human awed in the face of the God. Thus, we turned towards the audience simply, offering the final words 'The unexpected God makes possible and that is what has happened here today'.*

There was no place for an actor who only turned on their attention for their own scenes but switched off before and after. The actors never left the performance arena but remained in the grip of the tragedy throughout. Individual performers with specific roles would sometimes emerge from the chorus, only to be reabsorbed after their scene. The intention was to create an almost hallucinatory intensity that knitted performers and public in a kind of ritual celebration.

Within *The Bacchae*, Hart would inject roles and text, that were not a part of the original play by Euripides but corresponded to what he considered to be a necessary innovation that made the performance a truer reflection of those who were presenting it. A key figure, The Dreamer, was inserted into the play whose role was to comment and contrast the intensity of the tragedy as it inevitably unfolded. Dorothy Hart took on this role and has written about the gradual inclusion of material other than the original text of *The Bacchae*:

> 'In the beginning was the Word'. This was the backbone of the production. As the production grew and gave flesh to this backbone, the value of the non-script became recognised. Different members of the cast were encouraged to express their own meaningful associations with any part of the play ... The play had taken on the dimension of a dream, fusing Euripides' time with our time and all time ... the non-script consists of some 'addenda' originally spontaneous and now adapted and 'set', and also of some spontaneous material, new to each performance. This keeps the production in a permanently growing state and ensures that each performance is a cathartic ritual relating specifically to the present situation.
>
> (Dorothy Hart 'God is dead. Long live ...?' 1969)

Roy Hart also encouraged members of the group to introduce other elements into the play. A son of Pentheus was introduced, a kind of boyhood shadow of Pentheus the King. Richard Armstrong describes how he invented a scene based on the goddess Kali at Hart's request:

> He finally told me to write my own speech. And that the part that I was to play was the Indian goddess Kali. Now the Indian goddess Kali does not appear in *The Bacchae*. [...] I remember going to the library at the school where I was teaching and looking up who Kali was because I didn't know and basically taking out text from this stuff that I looked up, and I wrote a speech that was two pages long, and I handed it to Roy and he said 'That's fine, that's your part and that's your speech'. And it begun 'I am Kali, the life force' and it went on and of course Kali was the Indian goddess of violence and aggression – the life force. I always remember that this whole thing became a scene in *The Bacchae*.
>
> (Armstrong 2018).

In November 1968 Hart opened rehearsals to invited guests, including Frank Marcus who wrote the first review of this piece:

> The representation was non-realistic. Dionysus was played by three characters each embodying a distinct aspect of the god: Agave was a man. [...] Once again it was fascinating to trace the parallels of other contemporary theatrical investigations – not, let me hasten to add, a case of imitation or of cross-fertilization where Hart is concerned. These are the fruits of 20 years of lonely effort [...] But it is significant that the testing of ancient myths for modern validity is also an avowed aim of Grotowski. He too 'bounces a play like a ball against the wall'. But whereas Grotowski's actors are like emissaries from the audience confronting a common enemy i.e. the play, Roy Hart claims spiritual unity with Euripides—Even more striking is the affinity with the work shown recently at The Roundhouse under the direction of Peter Brook [*The Tempest*] and others. Here Mr. Brook may well have been influenced by Mr. Hart. [...] Above all the falsetto wheeze, cracked roars, *glissando* sweeps, and choral incantations conjured up the ghost of Artaud: the prophet of unreason. Mr. Hart has welded together a group of disparate individuals into a single body: their limbs intermingled like the tentacles of an octopus, the voices belonged to all. In an atmosphere of sectarian intensity Mr. Hart exercised the 20-headed monster of his creation. It was an enthralling but slightly menacing experience.
>
> (Marcus 1968)

The performance was extremely simple in its design and costumes were limited to simple rehearsal-style clothing. The women wore mainly leotards and tights, the men in tee shirts and short or long trousers. The only significant prop was a rope that the chorus used throughout the play and a piano that Hart used in some of the performances, notably at The Roundhouse, where it was mounted on a cart with wheels:

> The piano has been chosen as the only background orchestration other than the human voice, because it is part of the history of the group's training, and because it has a very wide set of associations for most people of European background. [...] The rope is the only other 'prop', chosen because it lends itself so particularly fluidly to the dream form our production has adopted. It binds and expresses throughout the production, taking the part of snakes, the ramparts of the city wall, and other active forms [...] only since using the rope in this production has the full richness of its associations with our method of

working been realised, as we seek to sound every strand in the length of our bodies.

(Dorothy Hart 'God is dead. Long live ...?' 1969)

Lighting was very simple and dependent on the space. Paul Silber would be responsible for lighting (The Roundhouse and The Place) but there were few light cues as such. Hart preferred the performance to take place in the round with spectators on all sides. This heightened the sense of collective ritual:

Kevin Crawford remembers: *Roy Hart didn't work on character as such in a direct way but he demanded a constant attention to how the characters and actions of the play found echoes in the personal and social lives of the performers. We were not allowed to forget that we too had murderous energies, that we too longed to leer at the women, that we too had the triple-headed Dionysus in us, bull, androgyne and avenger. We too were blinded by ecstasy like Agave and we too celebrated the unexpected. This continuing reference to self and society was bolstered up by the interventions and comments of The Dreamer, and, in rehearsal, the inclusion of moments of personal and ensemble expression that emerged spontaneously or through Hart's intervention. Each rehearsal and every performance demanded a kind of metamorphosis on our part, a readiness to sink down into the deeper, almost archetypal depths of ourselves in order to resurface, in a sense purified by the catharsis of the play. Person, actor and character in Roy Hart's conception were in powerful and ever-present dialogue, propelling us towards what he would term a full embodiment of a role.*

Hart's direction was not conventional. He had no overall staging plan that he had worked out on paper in advance. No outside collaborators were called upon at this point for the production. Hart used *The Bacchae* as a crucible to purify and strip his actors of their habitual personae. He would not hesitate to link both the individual psyche and the interpersonal chemistry within the group with a performance. For instance, just before the actors went onstage at Nancy for their premier performance in the World Theatre Festival in April 1969, he asked Hans Andrews to speak about a dream he had had the previous night. Listening to his dream and Roy Hart's connecting it to the forthcoming inaugural performance, constituted a bringing together of the participants and a consolidation of their collective power. Three professional dancers – Barrie Irwin, Derek Rossignol and Robert Harvey – helped mould the chorus into a compact and very disciplined unit. Using the rope as a primal symbol of capture and release, of conflict and containment, the chorus is intertwined with the principal characters and the unfolding drama. Kaya Anderson's notes to her script demonstrate the presence of the rope throughout. In the initial chorus she notes the movements of the chorus, sometimes with simple illustrations beside Vellacott's text, and the interjections of the character of The Dreamer:

'There's a brute wildness in the fennel-wands-	
Reverence it well. Soon the whole land will dance	*Taughten rope at angles*
When the god with ecstatic shout	*Definite Movements*
leads his companies out	
To the mountain's mounting height	
swarming with riotous bands	*Dancing wildly round with rope*
Of Theban women leaving	
Their spinning and their weaving	
Stung with the maddening trance	*Rope leader starts to disentangle rope, over Barrie's head, moving anti-clockwise*
Of Dionysus!'	
	Dot [abbreviation for Dorothy Hart] cue: 'Suffragette behaviour is forced upon the women'
	(Anderson 1969)

Early in 1969 Hart received the invitation he had been waiting for: to perform the premier of *The Bacchae* at the *Festival Mondial du Théâtre Universitaire* of Nancy in France directed by Jacques Lang, subsequently to become Minister of Culture under François Mitterrand. As Minister of Culture, Lang was instrumental in the large-scale development and support of theatre companies. Roy Hart Theatre was to benefit from this expansion in the 1980s as the company had by then installed itself in France. This festival, although named a student festival, was in fact the most influential event in France introducing new talents and tendencies and had already brought to an international audience the works of Grotowski, The Bread and Puppet Theatre (who had astounded audiences with their audacious use of giant puppets and their brand of political activism through spectacle), Pina Bausch, Robert Wilson, *Teatro El Campesino* and many other practitioners and troupes that were to have a seminal influence on European theatre for a generation. A makeshift name for the company was found, The Roy Hart Speaker/Singers, and a troupe of 24 actors made the journey to Nancy.

The Bacchae was performed from 24–27 April 1969 in the Grande Salle of the University of Nancy. The room was packed with an audience, both French and international, that was very curious about this new group. France had just lived through the student and workers' protests of May 1968, which had immobilised France in a long general strike and seen unrest in the streets. This protest movement challenged traditional French values and authority, and had ushered in a wind of change. Interest in new approaches to theatre and the role of theatre in society ran high. Despite the fact that some of the audience left during the show, it was on the whole received enthusiastically:

> A mesmerising and fascinating performance! This was yesterday's event of the day. Very probably it is 'the event' of the festival, the only culmination of real research that has been given to us to see, and above all to experience [...] Tragedy of human weakness in the face of a cruel and mysterious divinity, Euripides' play is presented as a dream. And it is indeed a dream into which we are invited to enter, awake, by the quasi-magic power of voice and gesture. The text here provides a basis for sounds, movements, expressions, which translate the struggle between conscious and unconscious in each character, in each actor, and finally – and this is the marvel! – in each spectator [...] Finally, above all else, there is the voice: whistles, roars, incantations, sounds which one might consider 'unbelievable', but which, indubitably, give rise to emotions, creating an atmosphere of unreason, a kind of hypnosis. The sounds are no more individual in expression than the movements: men take on women's voices, and vice versa, in order to symbolise the interchange between human beings [...] But the methodology has not only a psychological or psychotherapeutic value: at the threshold of the real and the unreal, it allows one to partake of a performance whose mystery, beyond even that which we see and hear, plunges into an unknown that is in each of us, and which disturbs us.
>
> (Borrelly 1969)

However, some commentators pointed out inconsistencies and paradoxes they had experienced while witnessing one of the performances at Nancy. Bernard Dort, a major figure in French theatre over several decades, put it this way:

> It is impossible to sit through the three hours of *The Bacchae* by the Roy Hart Speakers without feeling a stranger to the 'cathartic ritual' that is taking place before us, to this 'dream bringing together Euripides' time, our time and all time'. [...] In order to really understand them, we would need in our turn to enter into the group, also live out this dream where is conjured up 'the lines of action that predict the future social structure', be like them and with them.
>
> (Dort 1969)

Following the performances in Nancy the company renamed itself Roy Hart Theatre and continued working on its version of *The Bacchae* now called *The Bacchae presented as The Frontae*. This title, a wordplay (Backeye becomes Front-eye), reflected the by now deconstructed version that the company was performing: language too was presented back to front. On 21 September Dorothy Hart wrote:

> Yesterday Roy told me that he wished to cut out the first part of *The Bacchae* and start from the entrance of Pentheus, and that instead of being a dreamer, I should now be a story-teller amongst children.
>
> (Dorothy Hart 'Dot's Visualisation' 1969)

Dorothy Hart visualised new scenes, based on non-verbal dramaturgy and text that would be the structure for a revised beginning to the play and also prefigure the company's next production. Not all of this was included in this version of *The Bacchae* but it heralded the drive on the company's part to shift from a classic text-based production to a more loosely devised style of theatre-making.

On 24 October 1969 *The Bacchae–The Frontae* premiered in England at The Place, the London Contemporary Dance Centre. At the Festival of Nancy, Hart had already played with the structure of the play by sometimes starting a performance at the beginning, or the middle, or even the end of Euripides' play. But at The Place he went a step further. Hart had often used gibberish as a key to freeing up the vocal range and the imagination of the performer. In *The Bacchae–The Frontae* the actors were required not only to speak gibberish as they progressed forwards through the play's trajectory but they also had to do it backwards, playing the scenes in a reverse order but meticulously true to each detail of physical and vocal scoring. Hence the very 'back to front' pun in renaming the play. At this performance, musical instruments apart from the piano were introduced for the first time. Dorothy Hart commented: 'tonight's performance will be the first in which musical and other instruments are used, as an extension of the body's ability to express itself' (Dorothy Hart notes on the production 1969).

In his review 'New View of *The Bacchae*' in *The Times*, Michael Billington wrote:

> Anyone who has faithfully followed the experimental theatre troupes whose work has been seen in London during the past two years must have been struck by one thing: the extent to which their methods and approach overlap. [...] As an experiment it had a lot in common with Peter Brook's version of *The Tempest:* the same exhaustive attention of a single phrase, the same emphasis on non-verbalised sound and the same attempt to mould a group into a single entity. It was, in fact, extremely impressive as a demonstration of disciplined communal theatre and such incidents as the death and rebirth ritual, with myriad hands fluttering like leaves in a breeze, were handled with delicate precision, [...]. My sole doubt is a familiar one, [...] we have, in fact, to rely on old fashioned verbal theatre to tell us what a play is actually about and to provide us with the necessary background to enjoy experiments in psychodrama of this kind.
>
> (Billington 1969)

The company continued to rehearse and fashion the play during the autumn, while it prepared for what was regarded as a run of important performances. During this period Roy Hart was often absent owing to his increasing success as a soloist in music theatre pieces written specifically for his remarkable vocal abilities: Hans Werner Henze's *Versuch über Schweine/Essay on Pigs* (1969), Stockhausen's *Spiral* (1969) and Maxwell Davies' *Eight Songs for a Mad King*, in particular, which toured substantially during the autumn of 1969 (see **Chapter One**). Richard Armstrong remembers how members of the company began to assume more active roles in directing the play:

> There were scenes in that Roundhouse show which we directed ourselves because Roy was away a lot and I think he told me to get cards with letters on

> them which I painted myself and that was 'The moment of greatest peril coincides with the moment of greatest hope'.
>
> (Armstrong 2018)

Reviewer John Abulafia was invited to a rehearsal directed by Hart in November:

> Roy Hart plays a very high note on the piano, and a girl called Anna [Allen] tries to copy the pitch by screeching as high as she can. Then Hart plays the note higher: Anna follows. They go higher and higher, with Hart insisting on her hitting the notes accurately. The range of her voice, and also it seems, her body and her mind, are stretched to what seems impossible limits [...] she makes a variety of noises; high, low, loud, soft, and each is an accurate portrayal of an emotional state to which the rest of the group responds. She is Dionysus and they are the Bacchae—I have never seen anyone 'let go' on stage as she did—Roy Hart himself is single minded and perceptive. He has a powerful personality, and inspires confidence. He dominates proceedings but says little. There is little he does not know about acting and direction—I have only one reservation—at no time in the rehearsal did I hear the word 'audience'. I do not think what I saw would be half as impressive in a theatre.
>
> (Abulafia 1969)

Roy Hart Theatre performed *The Bacchae* from 15–21 December 1969 at The Roundhouse in Chalk Farm, a venue well-known in the circles of avant-garde theatre, and where companies like **The Living Theatre** premiered their works.

The Living Theatre based in New York City was founded in 1947. It is the oldest experimental theatre group in the United States. For most of its history it was led by its founders, actress Judith Malina (1926–2015) and painter/poet Julian Beck (1925–85). From its conception, The Living Theatre was dedicated to transforming the organisation of power within society from a competitive, hierarchical structure to one based on cooperation and communal expression.

The play was now called *Language is Dead–Long Live the Voice (based on the Bacchae)*. These performances were to be the last as Roy Hart pursued even further his dismantling of the linear narrative of the play. In the performances at The Roundhouse, Hart took advantage of an upright piano that was on a barrow with wheels and would 'direct' from the piano much as he might do in a workshop session, using the piano as a tool for communicating his indications of tempo, volume, silence and rupture. On occasions the piano would be wheeled around by him with help from several of the actors, describing huge arcs of a circle on the immense floor of The Roundhouse, as the maenad chorus followed in exultation. The programme note for these performances summed up Hart's intentions as a director and his expectations of the effect the play might have on the audience:

> [Hart] aims not to entertain, but to encourage each performer (and through the performer those in the audience watching him) to dare to expose the growing, groping self as it reaches out to wider experiences, rather than to show a section of the self that has been refined and limited as in conventional theatre... Hart encourages his performers to base their work on an inner self-respect, purged of egotism, and to respect each other's discoveries so that they can adapt to constant change in the production.
>
> (Dorothy Hart notes on the production 1969)

Hart believed firmly that the actor needed to respond in the moment to every impulse within the ensemble but also to events offstage or even outside the auditorium. A strident cough from the audience might solicit an ironic echo from the actors, an ambulance siren's tonal call might be picked up and developed into a polyphonic chorus. This attention to the moment made each performance a unique event, closer to a workshop or studio experience, that might almost be an initiatory experience for the audience.

Occasionally the spell of the play upon the actors was so deep that it felt like a re-enactment of some ancient rite and they were sped back in time. A curious event at one of the performances at The Roundhouse was particularly marked by Kevin Crawford.

> Kevin Crawford remembers: *Once, during a performance at the Roundhouse, a young man precipitated himself on to the stage, so strong was the subterranean call of this rite-like atmosphere. In astonishment we continued the play, but now incorporated this new actor into our performing body. He too became Pentheus and experienced onstage the temptation of watching the maenads at their secret*

> *ceremonies, and he too became their victim and was dismembered at their hands. The final curtain call of this performance was particularly poignant and strangely uplifting: as if I had taken part in a religious event or ritual, a strong catharsis of spirit, highlighted by the inclusion of an anonymous audience member, who shared this ritual with us. At that moment this seemed to symbolize for me the intense devotional and transformative atmosphere of Hart's approach to theatre.*

The Roundhouse performances received substantial interest and were reviewed extensively. Herbert Kretzmer of *The Daily Express* wrote 'Stunning – this Trip with the Human Voice':

> Watching it is like chancing upon a group therapy session in full cry. Rejecting the repressive and limiting cadences of traditional languages, they croak, scream, cry like seagulls, sing sweetly, and shout hoarsely. The impact and the insight are sometimes stunning. I have never seen actors giving quite so much of themselves. Anyone interested in new directions should see the Roy Hart Theatre, who are at the Roundhouse until the end of the week. It's not so much a performance as a trip.
> (Kretzmer 1969)

Nicholas de Jongh for *The Guardian* was more measured:

> (Hart's) Roundhouse production is very loosely based on Euripides' *The Bacchae*, and has become a sequence and demonstration of sound and energy, a representation of death and rebirth: the emphasis being on regeneration and ecstasy, the Bacchic intoxication luridly brought to prolonged life. The snatches of Eliot and Lorca accompanied by crude music is the only extraneous point in an evening in which technique is superbly in evidence: it was wrong for catcalls to come when an actor said 'the empty vessel makes the loudest sound' but there was a touch of justice.
> (de Jongh 1969)

The performances at The Roundhouse marked the end of Hart's engagement with *The Bacchae*. The company had in a sense exhausted its potential for transformation and deconstruction. It had served its purpose as a vehicle, but now the company began to look elsewhere for inspiration. The burgeoning creativity of some of its more experienced members was to take a more central role, as Hart continued to concentrate on his solo career and gave more responsibility to individual members of the company.

AND

and was produced in 1972 by Roy Hart Theatre and was a culmination of several years of theatrical experimentation and prior productions (*The Singer and The Song*, *Birthday* and *A Song of the Mind*, that were performed in The Cockpit Theatre, London and at the Madrid Second International Theatre Festival the previous year as well as *The Crepuscular System*, *Nexus*, *Huanacu* and *Watanka* amongst others). *and* marked a synthesis of these productions, a theatrical form that sprang from studio explorations and that was to a large degree conceived and directed not by Roy Hart personally but by four senior members of the company: Dorothy Hart, Vivienne Young, Robert Harvey and Richard Armstrong. Armstrong recalls: 'I believe Vivienne and I chose the title *and* with encouragement from Roy. We decided it should be the smallest and most used word in the English language, and that it should be lower case' (Armstrong 2018).

Whilst rehearsals often took place under the watchful eye of Hart, the main artistic vision was that of these four directors. Hart's role was

Figure 3.2 The chorus of *and* in performance 1972, image courtesy of Ivan Midderigh, RHT Photographic Archives.

limited to ensuring that the four directors managed their own artistic differences, thereby maintaining a healthy working space for the sixteen-member cast. Scenes included in *and* were directly salvaged from these previous productions, and featured some studio exercises that were now taking a theatrical shape. It was a fierce blend of the burgeoning creativity of its four directors and the maturing performance skill of the cast.

> A new performance we called *and*. This seemingly simple name was intended to invoke larger ideas that Roy and the group had been developing. The program described it thus: 'It is not acting in the sense of 'illusion' but of containing the overflowing cup of God 'and' the Devil'. The title was that three letter everyday word linking those two mighty opposites, and it pointed to the middle ground of Abraxas. The sixteen core performers wore simple costumes and went with bare feet. For many people *and* was the definitive Roy Hart Theatre performance. [...] the French press perceived it as a new form, naming it *le théâtre du cri,* though the British press ignored it.
>
> (Pikes 2019: 134)

The company now had an engrained ethic of disciplined ensemble work, and had expanded its vocabulary to include polyphonic a capella singing, the introduction of musical instruments and increasing physical and choreographic plasticity thanks to the regular classes offered by members of the company and guest teachers at The Abraxas Club. Three of the founder members – Robert Harvey, Derek Rossignol and Barrie Irwin – all experienced dancers and choreographers, trained the company in early morning or evening sessions. At the same time the troupe was exposed to Mexican-born New York dancer and choreographer José Limón's technique through Hebe Rosa from Montevideo and to the Martha Graham technique taught by Shelley Lee from The Place, London. All these classes took place in the various spaces at The Abraxas Club. Rehearsals primarily were scheduled in the evenings and weekends and were often very long, demanding endurance and patience from the cast. A smaller group of actors was brought together for this production as Roy Hart Theatre began to trim the numbers involved in productions based to some degree on its budgetary means, and took into account the skills and availability of its pool of performers. Two musical instruments were onstage, a clarinet and a drum.

One of the most memorable moments of *and* was called The Magic Chord. This scene, born directly from studio improvisation guided by

Hart, involved the cast grasping each other in a tight writhing group, bodies facing into the centre, but faces sometimes twisted outwards, producing an ear-splitting cacophonic sound that would last for some long minutes, seemingly with no end in sight. As the bodies and voices hurled themselves ever deeper into The Magic Chord, the actors seemed to be expelling every last breath from their bodies in a grotesque and ecstatic final scream. The scene's climax achieved, they melted to the floor, apparently drained and empty. Given that this scene was played twice a night on tour sometimes it was less primal than it might have seemed. Richard Armstrong recalls:

> I think Roy instigated, you could say in a way he directed that Magic Chord idea but it wasn't based on making theatre it was more based on 'Make sound for as long as you can, until you die' […] By the time we were doing it in Spain we were sort of acting it. […] It went on a long time but you kind of paced yourself. And then people would look at each other for the collapse. So the collapse didn't really come out of total exhaustion.
>
> (Armstrong 2018)

What had initiated as a studio experience that was totally authentic and demanded unhesitating engagement to the point of extreme personal exhaustion (it could last with undulating crescendos for up to half an hour) had now taken on a more controlled form, with a relatively short time span and a series of physical and vocal markers that enabled it to be repeated and presented in public. In a similar way other experiments in studio were fashioned into discreet units and then linked either through movement or sound.

and had very few words. It was a composition of bodies and sounds. A pre- or post-verbal oratorio where the body was a pulsing living entity, and the 16 actors occupied the stage with a surplus of kinetic energy. But above all, it was a compressed envelope of sound, ranging from the pure polyphonies of Handel's Hallelujah Chorus drilled through by the piercing screams of a raging woman, from guttural rhythmic chants to a haunting voice accompanied by the clarinet. It had no storyline as such, rather it was a succession of powerful scenes that arranged themselves more through choreographic and compositional logic. Their modulation corresponded to kinaesthetic, musical dynamics. The expression was resolutely not based on a textual form but on the appeal and plasticity of the body and voice liberated from the apparent restriction of the word. And yet some key phrases were given centre stage. Once again, the staging and costumes were minimal. The company wore tightly fitted clothing of various bright colours. The only props were yards of large white sheets of paper that would be painted with the words 'The Moment of Greatest peril corresponds with the Moment of Greatest hope'.

> Kevin Crawford remembers: *Performing and was in many ways an exhilarating and satisfying experience. It lasted just over an hour and had no wasted or dead time. The cast was on stage throughout, and even the few solo moments required intense listening and presence from the chorus. The building blocks of the show had been assembled in an interlocking series of scenes that spoke their own logic in space and time. It was primarily a kinaesthetic experience, a journey through sound by a totally committed group of performers, who had achieved a high degree of trust and were attuned to each other. Our version of Handel's Hallelujah Chorus that Robert Harvey had rehearsed with us was an example. It started with us singing the chorus as faithfully as possible to the original intention of the composer. Robert Harvey conducted. Faintly at first, then steadily stronger there could be heard a distant shrieking, but there was no sign onstage of where these sounds, in total contrast to the jubilatory tone of the chorus, came from. The screams now became stronger and stronger, and there emerged a relatively slight figure, Nadine George, whose cries accelerated, gradually topping the crescendo of the oratorio. Nadine began to physically invade the singers' space. There resulted a short but tumultuous struggle between the soloist and the choir, until an even more strident shriek from the seemingly maddened Nadine finally overcame the harmonic unity of the choir, which collapsed in disarray. Playing this scene, often twice a night (and sometimes three times, when we would have to perform before the censor – obligatory in those times under General Franco's dictatorship) required a total commitment on our part: there was no place for sparing our energy or 'marking' the scene. The energy, concentration and intense ensemble cohesion required from us meant that, despite tiredness, we would complete an evening of performance feeling uplifted and refreshed psychically.*

Other company members remember elements of performance and their origins. Nadine George recalls her role in The Hallelujah Chorus:

> I think it was conceived as something very, very important. That Hallelujah Chorus and me as the resister, the child, that was resisting authority, that was trying to break through to something else, through the scream, which comes

> back right to Alfred Wolfsohn, it goes right back to the root of the work in the first world war, and the screams of the dying soldiers put in a modern context.
>
> (George 2020)

Three Conductors was another scene from *and* that Paul Silber remembers:

> As the name implies, three musical conductors, in a triangular formation, are each facing their own group of actors or 'orchestra'. The triangle arrangement allows the conductors to see each other for coordination, rhythm effects etc. A code of hand signals by the conductor informs the 'orchestras' of the required sounds.
>
> (Roy Hart Theatre n.d.)

Another company member, Ian Magilton, said of *and*:

> I think it was important ... because it was successful, it travelled a lot, it toured well more than *The Bacchae*, for example. I think it had an abstract nature that was more to do with the mood of the time: not necessarily the kind of theatre I would want to do now. I think it was particularly to do with Vivienne and Richard coming from art school, and they were immersed in this kind of art. There were very many abstract images like Beauty and The Beast and Looking for a Victim. It gradually became a more and more well-made collage over the years.
>
> (Magilton 2019)

and received in many ways a jubilant reception particularly in Spain, a country still under the fascist heel of General Franco, where every city would require a performance for the censor before the company were exposed to the general public. Since the primary concern of the censors was that there was no political provocation and no nudity, these run-throughs for the censor posed no problem. Although Hart avoided political activism in any direct form, he maintained that his work and its expression as practiced by his company was a pathway to individual and social transformation and, as such, a vector for political change. *and*'s message was a subtle one, but it also proclaimed freedom in another way, and was subversive in its depiction of liberation through physical and vocal abandon. The audience responded spontaneously to this explosion of personal and ensemble power, where narrow authority seemed to be overthrown: bouquets of roses flooded the stage amid cheers and standing ovations. Its reception in England was more muted, but it did gather interest from reviewers and theatre directors alike. The impact of *and* in Spain inspired several young actors to join the company and attracted intense interest in Hart, his company and his teaching, including extensive interviews for *Primer Acto* magazine.

However, the performance of *and* that attracted the most high-profile polemic was at the *Théâtre des Nations* festival in Paris on 18 April 1972. The ten-day event at the *Théâtre Recamier* was hosted by Jean-Louis Barrault, an immensely influential figure in French theatre at the time, renowned for his physically expressive acting style, epitomised in the film *Les Enfants du Paradis*, and his courageous support of the student protests of May 1968. Barrault had brought together such luminaries as Peter Brook and his *Centre International de Recherche Théâtrale* (CIRT) and Jerzy Grotowski as well as groups from Japan, Los Angeles, Mexico and France in an attempt to 'redefine theatre' in a post-May 1968 Paris. The event attracted a young and enthusiastic public as well as strong coverage from foremost critics. Roy Hart commenced with an extract of *Biodrame* as a prologue before the company emerged onstage and presented a version of *and*.

However, the public was divided in their reaction. Clara Silber reported one scene to Noah Pikes:

> Dorothy Hart was extraordinary in the singing lesson she gave herself. She sang 'I love my body' with increasing vigour and conviction as the booing intensified. She was standing in an open *plié*, her hands on her thighs, looking beautiful and strong, a wild woman in the truest sense.
>
> (Pikes 2019: 136)

During the performance some of the public left including Jean-Jacques Gauthier, a leading critic for *Le Figaro*, who subsequently wrote:

> Their technique is faultless; superb the manner in which their evolutions are patterned; the positioning, the production in all its details, the staging, the attention to setting and focus of awareness, are simply admirable [...] these young men in jeans, these young girls in dresses of all different colours but of a great simplicity, with effects of coloured spotlights, moving in a violent rhythm and in a manner which is always aggressive – an aggressiveness which they admit to be voluntary ... – are going to mime all the known actions of all the animal species; and this whilst producing cries, screams which are very shrill, cries which

are prolonged, terrifying, deafening [...] As if the ideal of the humanist of 1972, the ideal of those individuals who claim to be members of the intelligentsia, to have sensibility, art and culture, was to return to the level of beast and madman.

(Gauthier 1972)

Another commentator C. Backès-Clément saw the performance from a different angle:

But beyond song, pushing further the effects of the fascination of pure voice, the Roy Hart Theatre performance goes as far as madness. It is a performance of cries, shrieks, of modulations; not a word is pronounced except for words without sequence of such grotesque coherence that they merge into the insignificance of onomatopoeia. However, these excessive sounds, which produce in the spectator either a fascinated enjoyment or an extreme irritation, produce events, acts, engender myths; the cry becomes madness, the voice becomes support of delirium, the performance becomes unbearable and the ideological space of represented theatre is broken [...]This echo of the origins which makes itself felt before us, in the evocation of the 'horde', in the simulated presence of the new-born baby, in the loss which the child feels and in its deep distress, is at the meeting-point where the voice alone, apparently liberated from the constraint of meaning, finds it on the Other Stage: in the presence of the unconscious.

(Backès-Clément 1972)

and toured extensively in Spain, France, Switzerland and the United Kingdom throughout 1972. In Switzerland the company was sometimes referred to as *le théâtre du cri* and it achieved a certain notoriety. *and* was performed for the last time on 22 March 1973 at the First International Festival of University Theatre in Tunis where it was coupled with *Biodrame*, a solo performance for Roy Hart. In Tunisia Hart, brought up as a Jew, found himself surrounded by an Arab Muslim population and did not hesitate to engage wholeheartedly in a dialogue with the predominantly young festival organisers and the public. This was typical of his commitment to reach out beyond his own cultural background to others from diverse ethnic and societal contexts.

and probably achieved a high point in Hart and his company's theatrical experiments based on a collage of scenes, and a through-line that was shaped more like a musical or choreographic composition. From thence forward he would increasingly collaborate with writers mainly from Europe, who would adapt existing works or create original ones according to his vision. Words onstage were to become an increasingly vital vehicle for Hart as he shifted from a predominately sound-oriented world to plays that delivered their messages and story in a textual form as well as through images and soundscapes.

> It must be said at the beginning, that this dangerous and exciting journey into the 8-octave voice, that is to say, into sound, has been undertaken with the primary aim of discovering the source of the word, to which my theatre is returning.
> (Roy Hart programme note for concert by ORTF 1972)

BIODRAME

Roy Hart company member, and Pantheatre founder Enrique Pardo described Hart on stage:

> He was as charismatic as you could make it [...]. I have seen quite a few performers since and I have never seen anything as impressively charismatic as his presence on stage. [...] The moment that most impacted me was when he performed *Biodrame* – because there he was [...] actually saying what he thought about his work and about his ambitions, again ethical ambitions, of his relationship to his own body, to the public etc.
> (Pardo 2019)

Biodrame was written as a solo piece specifically for Roy Hart by **Serge Béhar**, and premiered in 1972 at the *Journées du Théâtre des Nations* organised by **Jean-Louis Barrault** at the *Théâtre Recamier*, Paris.

Serge Béhar (1925–2002) was born to Sephardi parents in Urfa, Turkey. After studying in Istanbul he fought alongside the Free French forces in Beirut, where he subsequently studied medicine, before moving to Paris and becoming a specialist in pneumology in 1950. From here onwards he led a double career as doctor and playwright. His medical background and his research into breathing and the voice led him to look at theatre through the physiological and psychological workings of the human body guided by its visceral emotions. A familiar figure in avant-garde theatre in Paris in the sixties and seventies, he collaborated

> with leading directors, in particular Jean-Maire Serreau and André Perinetti, who directed several of his plays. In 1975 he was named President of Freemasons in France. See CNES *Le repertoire des auteurs de théâtre*: http://www.repertoire.chartreuse.org/auteur515.html.
>
> **Jean-Louis Barrault** (1910–94) was a foremost French actor, mime and director. His reputation was firmly established through his role as a mime in the film *Les Enfants du Paradis* (1945) directed by Marcel Carné. As a militant supporter of the student protests in May 1968, he opened the Odeon Theatre to student occupation, for which he was forced to resign his post as director. He met Roy Hart in Paris in 1970 and subsequently came to see rehearsals at The Abraxas Club in London. The *Journées du Théâtre des Nations* aimed to bring theatre back to its origins, the body, and in this sense he saw Roy Hart's presence as emblematic of a return to the roots of the actor's voice.

Up to this point Hart had mainly experimented with texts from a variety of authors and poets in English although he had also performed in German with *Versuch über Schweine* but *Biodrame* was to be the first of a series of plays written for him and his company by Serge Béhar in French.

Hart performed *Biodrame* between 1972 and 1974, and recorded it for the ORTF [the French national radio channel at the time]. He performed it in French and this signified a shift in his use of language in performance. In general Hart performed *Biodrame* on an open stage or floor without decor, props or music, with the audience sitting close to him. He wore everyday clothing, monochrome shirt or roll neck jumper with lightweight trousers. Later he wore what was referred to as a white jumpsuit. There were little or no light cues and the intention was to make the performance as concentrated as possible on the words, sounds and gestures of the soloist. Sometimes he used *Biodrame* or sections of it as an introduction to another piece, for instance at the *Théâtre des Nations* in April 1972, he performed the first sections of *Biodrame* by himself on stage, and when he reached the word '*schizophrénie*' the company as a whole invaded the stage and took over with their performance of *and*. He subsequently performed the whole piece towards the end of the *Théâtre des Nations*, by which point the company had left for a tour in Switzerland.

Biodrame is a dramatic poem in seven sections:

I Entrance onstage
II Birth of acting
III First appearance
IV Play
V Freedom
VI Creation
VII Epilogue

Biodrame is an especially relevant marker in Roy Hart's evolution as an actor, as, through his collaboration with Béhar, he was given a text that allowed him to evoke the different stages of his personal and artistic journey. Hart wrote an accompanying essay entitled '*Biodrame*....is somewhat the story of my life' (Roy Hart 1973). In this personal essay Hart annotated lines of the text in each stanza as they reflected key moments in his life and research. These notes formed part of a letter to a French television producer in 1973 (name unavailable), in which Hart clarified and asserted his particular philosophy and how it affected both personal and artistic activity. This letter and his notes give us important insights into his attitude to his own voice and the importance he placed on his work in a wider political and social context.

Hart sums up what he understands to be the main theme of *Biodrame*:

> Through the use of the word, and its relevance to the voice and to the entire biological framework and mindscape that make up an individual, Serge Béhar, being a Doctor, Poet and Philosopher, wrote *Biodrame* in which he expressed in theatrical terms the central thesis of that which led us to study the cry. [...] Which means that man as an individual is the root of society. As a doctor, Béhar has understood that the political body expresses very clearly the biological body: and without a deep understanding of the inside man, both physically and spiritually, no actor or politician can express so-called objective ideas, except as a projection of this lack of internal knowledge.
>
> (Roy Hart '*Biodrame*....is somewhat the story of my life' 1973)

Biodrame evokes in robust images the intrinsic, intimate chemistry of actors, their bodies and voices. The language is stripped down, telegrammatic, visceral. It was designed to be a vehicle for Hart's expressive powers, giving him full rein to infuse it with his unique mix of extreme vocal timbres and powerful physical presence. In his interpretation the words took on a density of feeling and meaning that was palpable to the onlooker; they also became a trace of his own personal story.

Biodrame opens with the performer announcing their own advance towards life, apparently in all tranquillity, but not yet knowing where this life will lead them. Hart writes: '*Biodrame* is somewhat the story of my life. When in 1945 I left South Africa, to come to London, where I won a scholarship to RADA ... I did not realise I was in such a state of non-being' (Hart '*Biodrame*....is somewhat the story of my life' 1973).

Referring to the second stanza, Hart draws the comparison with his first singing lessons with Alfred Wolfsohn, his discovery of the multiple voices in himself and what he calls 'the human voice, as opposed to the specialised voice' (Roy Hart '*Biodrame*....is somewhat the story of my life' 1973). Already he reflects on 'the sense of hierarchy between the head and body, the visceral and intellectual functions' and posits theatre as a context for 'a creative synthesis of the extremes' (ibid.). The third stanza opens with the words: '*Maintenant que le jeu est commencé j'entends ma voix qui dit le texte le timbre de ma voix des cordes et des hautbois générateurs des sons de grognements d'un monde de musique*' ('Now that the play has begun I hear my voice speaking the text the timbre of my voice the string instruments and oboes generators of sounds of grunts of a world of music') (Béhar 1972). The poem moves on in a fury of physical and emotional interjections:

> ... *Je crie,*
> *je sens battre en moi*
> *mon coeur,*
> *mon sexe*
> *palpitations*
> *érections*
> *gigantesques*
> *sinus caverneux*
> *turgescents*
> *projection de sperme*
> *ou de mots ...*

[...I cry out, I feel beating in me my heart, my sex, palpitations, erections, gigantic, cavernous sinuses, turgescent, projections of sperm or of words...]

(Béhar 1972)

The fourth stanza is representative of how Roy Hart interpreted *Biodrame*, alternating moments of sheer sound with the text, sometimes colouring it with irony or wonder, shock or playfulness. For instance, before the words '*me feront crier au-delà de mes forces*' ('will make me scream beyond my own strength') he releases a piercing shriek, then says, accelerating, '*me feront crier au-delà de mes forces*' and follows it with a longer broken roar, somewhere between a strangled squeal and a raging bull; then repeats this time slowly '*me feront crier au-delà de mes forces*' (Béhar 1972).

He follows this with a series of very high, flutey sounds that evoke the frolics of neighing horses and introduces the next image: '*me feront rire a pleines dents comme un cheval qui hennit*' ('will make me laugh to bursting like a horse that neighs'). Hart's sounds are so telling in their almost descriptive quality that he then only needs to quietly and slowly mete out the words on their echo. Later when he arrives at the words '*Théâtre science de mon corps de ses reptations enfouies*' ('Theatre science of my body and of its buried writhings'), he sings the words slowly, first in a strong baritone, that gradually descends to a gravelly bass on the words '*reptations enfouies*'. As he speaks the lines '*Tandis que je marche sur scene la pensée accaparée par le texte*' ('As I walk on stage, my mind monopolised by the text'), he lends to these words an almost bland, ironic quality as if he sees before him the strutting actor. The stanza continues: '*par mes gestes et le timbre de ma voix*' ('by my gestures, and the timbre of my voice'). Here Hart repeats the words '*par mes gestes*' three times as he gesticulates onstage, before launching into a vocal improvisation in 'peep' sounds where we catch the words 'maman', 'papa' in a vertiginously high rendition of a baby crying, before landing in a sudden groan on the words '*des petits cris aigus jaillissent de chacune de mes cellules*' ('tiny shrieks spurt out of each of my cells') (Béhar 1972).

The fourth stanza ends with:

> L'amour
> et le rage
> issus de mes cellules
> sortis des dentrites
> de mes neuronses
> et brusquement
> mon corps
> dévoile jusqu'au secret
> le plus infime

de ma biologie
de mon existence intime.

[love and rage, born of my cells, coming out of the dentrites of my neurons, and suddenly my body unveils itself right up to the tiniest secret of my biology, of my intimate existence.]

(Béhar 1972)

The effect of Hart's combination of unbridled depictions in sound and his psychologically subtle colouring of the text was simply stunning. In a sense he performed a form of vocal mime, allowing himself to fully absorb the images Béhar offered up in this poem, and gave them ample expression in a way that was not simply a redundant transposition of the word into sound, but a complex play between the power of the word and the voice that embodied it.

In *Biodrame*, and in general in all his live performance work, be it music theatre or heightened textual expression, Hart opened up new perspectives for the voice in performance. He allowed us to see the potential of a voice that had acquired a fluency, power and subtlety over a large range. And, above all, he encouraged us to leave our fears, hesitations and resistances behind, and allow ourselves to invest fully in the rich network of meaning that words offer. His interpretations always looked for balance between vocal energy and verbal muscular manifestation of that energy. In that way he managed to light a path for the incipient actor, searching for, as he would put it, an 'embodiment of the word'.

The fifth stanza begins with:

Je ne veux plus être <u>captif</u>
hors de mes habitacles
je m'élance vers les voix
provenues des autres
captifs d'en face

[I do not want to be a prisoner any longer, out of my shell, I dash towards the voices, coming from the other prisoners, in front of me]

(Béhar 1972)

Hart's notes at this point articulate his awareness of having been captive in his head before discovering his own violence: 'this realisation gave me the courage of my humanity: real biological revolution which gave body to my need for communion with another individual' (Roy Hart '*Biodrame*....is somewhat the story of my life' 1973).

The stanza continues: 'A ton silence à ta distance à ton indifférence rèpond mon cri..........' (To your silence your distance your indifference replies my cry) and ends on a note of freedom and human exchange: 'Libéré de mon corps je te joue ton image tu me joue mon mirage nous sommes ensemble' (Liberated from my body I perform your image to you you play my mirage for me we are together) (Béhar 1972).

In the sixth stanza, Creation, the performer commences with 'Ce que je crie c'est l'amour' (What I shout is love). Hart's comment is revealing: 'My "cheminement" [path] of over twenty-five years since my first singing lesson is a biological process which organically fills the gap between theatre and reality... . My performance reflects how I make love and vice versa' (Roy Hart '*Biodrame*....is somewhat the story of my life' 1973).

The performer's journey seems to return to a new balance 'sans emphase' (without emphasis), where one can perform without masks, and, from hands that reach out and touch each other wells up the fire of creation: 'De nos mains qui se rapprochent à se toucher jaillit le feu de la creation'.

The Epilogue is a direct appeal to the other to join in this journey, before the performer vanishes:

> *Pour toi et moi je suis sorti hors de moi—*
> *mes yeux rivés sur mes songes—*
> *Avant de disparaître pour crier pleurer vivre avec toi...*
> *avant de disparaitre j'ai marché vers toi.*
>
> [For you and I, I have come out of myself—my eyes rivetted on my dreams—Before disappearing in order to shout weep live with you... before disappearing I walked towards you.]
>
> (Béhar 1972)

An unnamed reviewer of *Biodrame* when it was performed in Barcelona at *El Instituto del Teatro* in February 1973 wrote:

> *Biodrame*, which should be defined as a psychosomatic poem, is a meditation of the actor on his own organism, and at the same time on his relationship as an interpreter and an individual with the public. During the half-hour recital

(although this term doesn't go far enough) Hart awed the audience with the incredible expressive possibilities of his voice. For Hart does not only master all the possibilities of the human vocal range, from bass to soprano, but he is also able to emit various voices simultaneously. And it cannot be said that this acting is a virtuoso performance in search of effects; far from it, each sound, each modulation answered to a concrete expressive necessity.

(*Biodrame* 1973)

By 1974 Roy Hart was performing *Biodrame* in tandem with two other pieces for the company: *Ich Bin* by Paul Pörtner, a German playwright, and *Mariage de Lux* also written by Serge Béhar. These three works were performed as one complete show with three sections. The performance was called *Three Moods* and sometimes subtitled 'One French – One German – One Biological'. This triple billing was planned as a 'farewell performance' at the Open Space, London, 3–8 April 1974 – farewell as the company was already planning to depart for the Cévennes in the summer of that year – and at Theatre 11 in Zurich, 2–3 May. These performances also coincided with a particular intense period for the company as a number of members gradually gave up their own apartments to live in a more communal way in preparation for the imminent departure for France and a community-based life that awaited them there.

L'ECONOMISTE

L'Economiste, like other works by Roy Hart Theatre company, had a complex evolution. This work would prove to be final work by the company under Roy Hart before the tragic accident that took the lives of Roy Hart, Dorothy Hart and Vivienne Young. The accident occurred during the tour of this work (as described in **Chapter One**), so the tour was completed by the company at a later date, with different company actors taking on the roles played previously by the deceased.

By the summer of 1974 Roy Hart and the company had already made its final performances of *Three Moods* at *Teater Elf* in Zurich as well as the farewell season at the Open Space and the first seven 'pioneers' had begun installing themselves at Malérargues in the French Cévennes region. This was to be its future base and home to the now 49 members of Hart's company. Meanwhile Serge Béhar had written to Roy Hart that he was writing a new piece for him and the company. This

Figure 3.3 *L'Economiste* 1975, image courtesy of Ivan Midderigh, RHT Photographic Archives.

was immensely exciting news for Hart and he awaited this work impatiently. Béhar had already written *Biodrame* for him and had allowed another play *Mariage de Lux* to be used freely by the company, and Hart felt he was the writer closest to his work and vision. In addition Béhar was writing in French, the language that would now be the medium for the company in their adopted country.

The original play that Béhar proposed to Roy Hart was called *Le Café de Flora*. Vivienne Young described the first meeting between Roy Hart, Dorothy Hart, Paul Silber and herself with Serge Béhar when he presented the new play:

> Serge told us of a play – *Café de Flora* – which he said was written for us. The fact that he also mentioned showing it to one other actress already with a view to her performing Flora – and the fact that he had not told us at all that it existed – made us feel sure it was not actually written for us – having read the play and finding it impossible for us to perform we went to Malérargues, where we spent four days of concentrated work and study writing a love letter to Serge.
>
> (Young 1975)

Dated 17 December 1974, Hart's letter begins: 'Dear Serge, this is not a lecture. It is a love-letter, an informed love-letter. I say that because I know that at times it may sound like a lecture' (Roy Hart 1974). The letter continues with a detailed account of Vivienne Young's dreams following this first reading. Summing up his comments on the dreams and their significance to *Le Café de Flora* Hart asserts: 'For us to be able to work on *Café de Flora*, we need to redirect consciously this play' (ibid.). The second part of the letter is an impassioned and detailed critique of the play with a plan for revisioning it:

> From the very beginning we wish to use the voice to reveal different levels of consciousness, as for instance Maurice, from his first 'moan' makes a pre-verbal statement, which he hopes will lead to the embodied word and not to the chattering of an idle brain which has lost all contact with its gut – The theme of the play should be the struggle, the struggle of the 20th Century, of the conscious voice which is trying to express itself (Maurice or Serge as performed by Roy) against projections, instruments[...] We are never allowed to tell a story which does not return to biblical imperatives. In other words it is not allowed to tell a story without a moral.
>
> (Roy Hart 1974)

Translated into French, this letter was then read directly to Serge Béhar in his Paris home on 20 December by Lucienne Deschamps in the presence of Roy Hart, Dorothy Hart, Vivienne Young, Pascale Ben and Paul Silber. Serge Béhar immediately began rewriting. Shortly afterwards he was to send his revised play, now to be called *Les Lumières de l' Été*. There followed an intense period of rewriting, editing and composition. This process was shared between Hart and his closest collaborators, based at this point in Switzerland, with the company members already installed in their new residence in the south of France, and the members who were still in London, managing The Abraxas Club. During a whirlwind two weeks, Serge Béhar reviewed his play with the input from these three centres, and on 17 January delivered what was to be the basis for the final version.

In contrast to works like *The Bacchae*, *and*, or *Mariage de Lux*, where the performance score only gradually emerged from long hours of studio experimentation and improvisation, the work on *Les Lumières de l'Ete* was more heavily based on an existing text and sought to mould it to the dramatic and philosophical constraints that Roy Hart and the company wished to impose. For the first time Hart wanted a play that would reflect his belief system and how he envisioned its unfolding. Perhaps this also came about because of the physical distances between the compact group in Switzerland, the burgeoning numbers already in Malérargues, its future centre, and the team still occupied at The Abraxas Club in London. Collective rehearsals were not possible so the attention was focused on the written material, that would be the skeleton for the performance. But it was perhaps also a reflection of Hart's need to return to the word and review his company's reputation as *le théâtre du cri*.

During this period of writing, a studio space in Malérargues was being completely renovated in preparation for the imminent arrival of Hart and collaborators from Switzerland. The majority of the members still in London arrived very soon after, so rehearsals were able to start on the play by February. By this time, its name had changed once again, to *L'Economiste*:

In interview, company actor Kaya Anderson said:

> Roy's idea of calling it *l'Economiste* was that we have to work out what we are doing, how long it's going to take, and where it can be performed, so there is economy in this way of thinking, that's why it became the *L'Economiste*'.
>
> (Anderson 2018)

Another actor, Ian Magilton, offered a slightly different memory:

> My understanding of why it became *L'Economiste* was because the main bulk when we finally got to rehearsing was done here in Malérargues under extreme economic duress, thermic duress ... Everything seemed to be about the economy. I think Roy said 'We should call it *L'Economiste*'.
>
> (Magilton 2020)

L'Economiste tells the story of Flora and Maurice: Flora is a young singer who works in the Café de Flora, Maurice is a poet and visionary. '[He] has persuaded Flora to leave her upper middle-class family to live with him in the café' (Dorothy Hart 1975). The other major figures are the Technarch, a 'macho' figure, representing the dangers of a world driven by technological prowess, and Justine. Justine is a servant in Flora's family and has watched Flora grow since childhood. She plays a complex role in the play, both *provocateur* and guardian angel. Constellating around these main characters is a chorus, who assume diverse roles: sometimes they are clients in the café, sometimes they embody Flora's family and worldly friends, and later in the play they transform into sinister masked men. Out of the chorus occasionally emerge characters who appear transiently. The opening scenes describe the relationship between Flora and Maurice, their closeness and conflicts. Maurice seems to be a dreamer and Flora wants be successful, entertaining the clients. Flora and Maurice spar over questions of money and recognition. Maurice argues for spiritual and ethical freedom. Flora is not yet able to fully recognise Maurice for who he is and accept their love. Maurice tells her a dream that foreshadows their future together. A future that will involve separation, loss and eventual reconciliation.

Flora's confusion and inner disquiet invites a malevolent energy, the clients becoming hideous, disfigured masked men who finally succeed in carrying Flora and Maurice away. Flora finds herself back with her family and worldly friends. Maurice is spirited away, held captive by the banks of a river. Flora's family try to win her back into the family fold, by rejecting Maurice. Flora resists, and seems to be winning, as she slowly finds her own voice, stripped of superficiality. Now Justine, playing her double role of guardian angel/*provocateur* offers her the possibility of meeting a prince charming who will cure all her woes. Flora accepts the invitation to meet the Technarch but soon finds him repellent and destructive. After the downfall of the Technarch, Flora understands that she wants to live, not die separate from Maurice. Once Flora has attained a new maturity, Maurice is able to release himself from bondage and return to her. They celebrate this return and Justine, who too has been released from her servitude, performs a marriage ritual for them, accompanied by the chorus, who embody their joy but also strike a note of deep seriousness in a final circle of chanting.

EVOLUTION OF THE TEXT

The textual changes from *Café de Flora* to *Les Lumières de l'Eté* and finally to *L'Economiste* are fully documented between *Les Lumières de l'Eté* and *L'Economiste* but unfortunately at the time of writing (May 2021) the authors have not been able to locate a copy of the original play – *Le Café de Flora*. However, based on the copies of the two plays mentioned above and the wealth of letters exchanged between the three centres of editing and rewriting, and extensive notes on the music for the show, we can piece together some of the more salient changes. Tracking the evolution of a RHT script from *Les Lumiere de l'Ete* to *L'Economiste*, we can see how the company gradually transformed the text to align with their vision. Structural changes involved the addition of a small orchestra and the importance given to the role of The Pianist who shadowed Roy Hart and conducted the orchestra. Several scenes and minor characters were introduced in *L'Economiste*: Les Deux Filles (the two women), Albert, Edith and Monsieur Martin. The text for Maurice changed considerably, becoming less hyperbolic and tighter, more poetic. Sometimes his text carried words that could be attributed to Roy Hart: 'Love is the name of every idea you dare to sing' (Béhar and Roy Hart Theatre 1975: 13) or Hart's words might appear in another character's text: 'Maurice is an actor who doesn't practice *divertissement*. That is why he hasn't performed in public for so many years' (ibid.: 14). Other striking changes involved the addition of new songs, the juxtaposition of two choirs in the confrontation between Flora and the Technarch and the editing of the final marriage scene, giving it a sober but celebratory tone.

PROGRAMME NOTES

Dorothy Hart in 'A Reality Dream' wrote: 'this play shows how Maurice and Flora slowly and painfully come to that point, moving in a mindscape where "dream" and "reality" have significantly undefined boundaries' (Dorothy Hart 1975). Dorothy Hart's programme notes trace the symbolic and psychological thread of the play through all its events and interactions. In conclusion she writes:

> The period of transformation has been completed. Balance has been established between the individual and the collectivity. Flora no longer needs to live only with Maurice; she will live with him and the clients, in their café of the world. Now, Justine unites them in a marriage ceremony that is at one and the same time a union and a guarantee of total individual liberty, an action that attaches and detaches. Flora, Maurice, Justine, the clients, the whole company, are finally united.
>
> (Dorothy Hart 1975)

REHEARSALS AND TOUR

Hart's commitment to *L'Economiste* was all the more pressing for him as it was to be a primary artistic statement of his company in their new home and country. Extensive tours in Austria and Spain were already planned, and it would therefore, he believed, launch them on their European career, having left England and its lacklustre support behind.

L'Economiste was in many ways a very ambitious project. It was the first time the company had formed a small orchestra from its own ranks. The instruments were: piano (Jonathan Hart), saxophone (Noah Pikes), trumpet (Stephen Moore), clarinet (Boris Moore), flute (Rafael Lopez Barrantes) and percussion (Jeremy Samuels). Although all of them had studied music, they had different levels of experience in playing professionally and had to dedicate many hours of rehearsal to creating an ensemble sound quality, and the ability to respond to subtle changes in interpretation from the cast. The choreographic elements in the play were equally challenging. As well as dances for specific songs like *Les Deux Filles*, it included a stunning medley of dances that ranged from a riotous can-can to a traditional Greek circle dance in 7/8 time: the whole sequence lasting over 15 minutes! Robert Harvey oversaw this aspect of the performance. Jonathan Hart speaks of how he worked with Roy Hart on composing one specific scene where Maurice tells a prophetic dream:

> He must have gone into the studio, on his own [...] he was actually doing something very simple on the piano with just octaves. He then showed me that, and then I went to the piano and started doing what he was doing and then he continued to improvise [...] His structure was based on vocal colours, vocal states rather than pitches. Me, on the piano, was gradually homing in on pitches, timing, fixed things, in relation to that [...] It was more like revealing together, or tuning into, or revealing the pith.
>
> (Jonathan Hart 2020)

Although the company now had a definitive script for *L'Economiste* and roles had been assigned, there was still a wealth of detailed work musically and choreographically to put flesh on the bones of the skeleton of the script. Most of the music was composed or arranged by the company, primarily by Jonathan Hart, Boris and Stephen Moore. In his programme note, Boris Moore reflects on the nature of music in general and how it is manifested in *L'Economiste*: 'Most of the music in *L'Economiste* that has been composed, emerged as composed music from the natural music of the words, of their significance and dramatic force' (Moore 1975).

Two pieces were based on existing scores by Mozart: a virtuoso rendition of arias from *The Magic Flute* sung by Jonathan Hart as he accompanied himself on the piano – this piece preceded Hart and the company's first entrance onstage – and a vocal arrangement by Stephen Moore of *Maurerische Trauermusik*, that was chanted by the chorus of masked men.

L'Economiste contained no less than 11 scored songs, but it also included many less formal moments of accompaniment and orchestration, particularly between piano and Roy Hart's voice. Recordings of rehearsals in Malérargues from spring 1975 illustrate the tight dialogue between piano and voice, between words and music. In one sequence Hart plays with a wide array of sound on the words *'La nuit est douce à vivre dans notre tanière de poésie'* ('The night is sweet to live in our den of poetry'). We hear double-stopping sounds like a deep organ on the words *'La nuit'*, which swoop up to a high bird-like call on *'douce à vivre'*, that transition through a multi-stranded voice to land on the words *'notre tanière de poésie'* sung almost operatically: immediately Hart repeats the words, as if he needs to make them more understandable. In Act III, accompanied by the piano, he sings a love song, this time a mixture of gentle melody, Sprechgesang (half melody, half speech) and leaping arpeggios that may break into fierce cries. Sometimes the piano leads the singer on, sometimes the two are finely balanced or the singer anticipates the piano, which follows almost in commentary.

The chorus too, whether it was as the customers, the masked men or the family, were strictly calibrated in their texts and their vocal orchestration. The musical density of the piece applied to every part of the soundscape: orchestra, voice, text. In particular, the two opposing choruses in Act II, Machine and Human Chorus, were precisely directed to point out the dramatic shifts in the scene between Justine, Flora and the Technarch.

The choreographic and spatial design was also demanding. Directed by Robert Harvey and Barrie Irwin, this included duets for Maurice and Flora, the Deux Filles as well as dances for a male chorus and the final ensemble dance medley. Robert Harvey writes in 'The role of dance in *L'Economiste*':

> Up till now, it has been difficult to allow ourselves the luxury of working on fixed choreographies. The nature of our work was such that strictly choreographed dances would have been incompatible with the fluid energies of our previous pieces: but these energies have now been harnessed and used, without (I think)

> falling into the trap of choreographic style, but express on the contrary the humanity of the singer/dancers.
>
> (Harvey 1975)

The first public showing of scenes from *L'Economiste* took place at the *Chapelle des Pénitants Blancs*, Avignon, in March 1975, followed by the formal premier at the *Théâtre d'Alès*, now named *Le Cratère*, on 12 April. The credits for this first version of *L'Economiste* attributed the Stage Direction (*mise en scène*) to Roy Hart, Richard Armstrong, Enrique Pardo and members of Roy Hart Theatre. Paul Silber was credited with the lighting and technical management; Barry Irwin and Robert Harvey were the choreographers.

An event at the beginning of the show in Alès is revelatory of Hart's attitude to performance and his insistence on 'being in the moment'. Paul Silber recounts it:

> Another time, it was for *L'Economiste* at the Alès Theatre and we had worked out with Robert (Harvey) a complex set of positions for our stools onstage and taped the stage with their exact places. Roy was onstage before and, without warning, he sent all the stools flying, so when we came back on we had to scurry around replacing the stools in their original positions.
>
> (Silber 2018)

The company continued to work on the play, and departed at the beginning of May for a two-week tour in Austria, the prelude to a longer season of performances in Spain. This was to be the international premiere of *L'Economiste*. The tour was made possible by Heiderosa Hildebrand, a member of the company at that time, who was a well-known director of an art gallery in Klagenfurt. Three performances were to take place: 7 May in the *Kunstlerhaus*, Vienna, 11 May in Klagenfurt and 15 May at Villach during the *Festival Spectrum'75*, that brought together public and professionals eager to see new trends in theatre. In addition workshops took place in Vienna. The programme notes were translated into German but the play remained in French.

> Kevin Crawford remembers: *My strongest memories of* L'Economiste *are of waiting in the wings with the rest of the cast before our first entrances while Jonathan Hart is alone at the piano singing his way through* The Magic Flute, *boding forth its arc of voices and archetypal characters. It is a prelude to the show that lets us all drop into a deep concentration so we can give our utmost in the next two hours.*

The masked men scene too was a powerful moment, a kind of sinister variation on the childhood game of statues. Gradually, with at first contained, then outright menace, we circled around Flora and Maurice: like wheeling obscene vultures we preyed on them until they fell to our maniac song and gestures. The dances at the end were always a moment of great release and satisfaction. The story between Flora and Maurice had run full circle and we were back at the café with a renewed sense of vitality and ease. In the final tableau we paced the stage in a perfect circle repeating the words 'day after day', as it if to remind ourselves of the repetition of life, that yet has to renew itself. This was especially poignant, when we performed this ending after the death of Vivienne, Dorothy and Roy.

The performances and workshops in Austria received on the whole a warm reception, and the company, after the rigours of a winter of intense rehearsal in Malérargues, enjoyed the spring and the stimulus of an audience. However, for its final appearance at Villach the reaction was mixed and a post-performance colloquium with the public proved to be conflictual. During this meeting Hart was questioned about his dominant position as leader of the company. A few observers criticised him for what they perceived to be his overbearing, manipulative role. This was refuted by Roy Hart and members of the company but the comments left their mark, and later in a meeting with the cast Roy made it clear these criticisms had hurt him. He was disappointed that after so long, certain commentators still mistook the level of commitment he demanded, from himself and those around him, for a desire to exert power over those persons. In this meeting Roy also allowed those of us present to have a little more insight into his own vulnerability as a man and artist. Paul Silber recalls this moment in Villach:

Villach [May 1975 a few days before fateful accident] was a very painful time for Roy. He was criticized for having created a group of performing monkeys. This hurt him deeply. Criticism had never been easy for him to swallow and this was particularly bitter.

(Silber 2018)

The reviewer for *Volkszeitiung Klagenfurt* wrote:

On the evening of the performance there were not only whistles and boos for this ensemble, which made the strongest impression of the festival on the reviewers, but also the opinion of a distinguished foreign participant that the RHT was 'fascist' because of its structure and working method – a very foolish comparison, unless one equates discipline, ambition and hard work with fascism.

(*Volkszeitung Klagenfurt* 1975)

Within less than a week of this review Roy Hart, Dorothy Hart and Vivienne Young were to make their final journey, their lives taken away by a fatal accident on a French autoroute near Fréjus. Paul Silber, the fourth occupant of the car, was wounded in the accident but went on to make a full recovery. However, the company showed proof of an extraordinary resilience in deciding to remount *L'Economiste* less than three months after its loss. In the original production Roy Hart had taken the role of Maurice, Vivienne Young played Flora, and Dorothy Hart and Lucienne Deschamps performed Justine as a duo. Richard Armstrong had been cast as the Technarch. In the remounted version, Richard Armstrong took on the role of Maurice and Elizabeth Mayer that of Flora. Lucienne Deschamps performed Justine alone and Paul Silber played the Technarch. This new version premiered on 13 August in the cultural centre of Saint Jean du Gard, and was followed by performances in Alès, Nimes and Montpellier. In 1976 this new *L'Economiste* toured on three separate occasions to Spain: Madrid, Valencia and Alicante. The performance at Saint Jean du Gard was reviewed by *Le Monde* under the title 'The Morality of Roy Hart Theatre':

> one hesitates to classify, to label, for one is present at something astonishing, [...] the whole philosophy of Roy Hart Theatre is effectively contained in *L'Economiste*. The play seeks to convey a morality: 'Every individual is indispensable. Every individual within the individual is indispensable, irreplaceable, [...] One cannot become an individual when one is afraid of being directed.' These are the principles which rule the community life of the forty members of Roy Hart Theatre at the Château de Malérargues. And it is by theatrical practice that they achieve intellectual, physical and moral equilibrium.
>
> (*Le Monde* 22 August 1975)

The *Le Petit Cévenol* critic saw the performance in Alès and echoed the above response, and went even further to describe the powerful innovations of this work:

> This performance has the rare merit of not leaving us indifferent [...] a strong show, very strong, at times almost untenable, which forces us to draw up from

> very depth of ourselves all our emotional resources [...]. Never have voices resounded in this way in this theatre, never has the scenic space been occupied with such care, such detail and intensity in order to release and to touch [...] we have the impression we are returning to the very sources of expression.
>
> (*Le Petit Cevenol* 1975)

Spanish critic and theatre theorist José Monleón had followed Roy Hart and his company from its first appearances in Spain, and had conducted extensive interviews with Roy. After seeing the second version of *L'Economiste* in Madrid, he wrote:

> If the Roy Hart Theatre has occupied a relevant position in modern theatre, it has not been because of its philosophy - even though this might be inseparable from its work – but because of the empowerment of the voice – as an inarticulate organic expression – as a revealing element of the reality that resists being buried by compulsions and clichés. It is in this line that it must insist, avoiding the danger of entrusting to the fable, the text, the thesis or the conventions, what was conceived as a direct confrontation of the actor with himself and with others through the liberation of the voice.
>
> (Monleón 1976)

4

PATHWAYS TO THE HUMAN VOICE

In the footsteps of Roy Hart and Roy Hart Theatre

PARADOXES AND PATHWAYS

In preparing a chapter on exercises arising out of Roy Hart's work and that of the company on the voice, and its application in theatre and music, we come up against a fundamental paradox. Roy Hart himself would have eschewed any attempt to codify or set down in writing his teaching or the specific 'exercises' he used. He relied, one might say, on an oral tradition to transmit his knowledge and skills to others in his company as he gradually empowered them to teach. As this book has amply demonstrated, in both studio and performance, Hart believed intrinsically in the value of 'being in the moment'. It followed that no two of his lessons or group sessions were the same, and he would deliberately test his students and company to ensure they were as committed as possible to each unique moment in time. He believed in thoroughly submitting to the needs of the student in a lesson, and this demanded a level of listening from him that one might qualify as listening in depth, his entire being at their service. He brought a great depth of concentration to diagnosing the myriad messages he was receiving from the students' sounds, bodies and faces in order to support them in summoning up the full force of their vocal potential. He taught therefore mostly by example, inviting his collaborators to tune in to their own deep intuition, so they could allow their students to conjure up

DOI: 10.4324/9780429266430-4

their own personal vocal pantheon. However, 'exercises', or it might be more appropriate to call them 'pathways', did surface. At no point, though, did Hart lose sight of the fundamental aim of his work: the freeing or liberation of the individual voice and its corollary in the personal and social experience of that person. An exercise therefore was only valid in so far as it served that purpose and would be revised continually to adapt to each person and each situation. His approach was not to adapt the person to a previously codified approach to the voice but to act as a medium, containing and provoking the full range of their voice. After his death, Roy Hart Theatre continued to expand on his teaching by further developing an approach that integrated body and psyche with the voice. A diversity of styles emerged as individuals within the company explored and made his approach more their own, reflecting their own skills and aspirations. The pathways proposed here therefore do not attempt to reproduce any specific 'exercise' that Hart offered, rather they reflect the transformations his legacy has achieved. One can be relatively sure that Hart would have been happy to see that his work was not being followed dogmatically but rather had given birth to a constellation of teaching approaches that still were in the gravity field he had established.

Digging deep into one's vocal strata is not something to be undertaken lightly and students are advised to dip into the following 'pathways' with due care and patience. Obviously if they can do so in the company of their peers with the guidance of an experienced teacher, they will be able to do so in security and can more easily process their experience in sharing it with others. Please remember therefore what your overall aim is in working through these sequences: *an exploration of your vocal material without judgement or an initial demand for an outcome.* Treat each journey with maximum concentration and be like a modern-day archaeologist, painstakingly turning over the layers of sound, with curiosity and fresh delight. Be alive to the echoes this work stirs in your personal life, include your dream self in this, and do not hesitate to reach out into related fields of philosophy and psychology to give depth and context to your experiences. You might want to read something of the work of C.G. Jung, for instance *Modern Man in Search of a Soul* (1955, first published in 1933), or *Man and his Symbols* (1968, first published in 1964), *Dream and the Underworld* by James Hillman (first published in 1979) and *Inner Work: Using Dreams and Active Imagination for Personal Growth* by Robert A. Johnson (first published in 1986) – all offer insights into the interplay of dream and waking life, symbols and the unconscious. Keep in mind that you are working with your voice, and that your voice expresses your own personal story as well as being a mirror of the culture you are born and living in, and connects to a repository of archetypal figures, reaching back into human and animal ancestry. You may have a very personal story that is wrapped into your vocal matrix. Soul, spirit and matter come together in exploring your voice. And sometimes silence too…

This work is based on a rejection of voice classification as male or female. There is fluidity of gender embodied in the work here and in the work of the company in its casting choices, such as in the double-casting of Kevin Crawford and Kaya Anderson as Ariel in their 1977 version of *La Tempête* (*The Tempest*) and Richard Armstrong as Clytemnestra and Jonathan Hart as Cassandra in Roy Hart Theatre's co-production with Talking Band, New York, on their version of *Furies* (1986).

This chapter includes a number of warm-ups and other exercises from Kevin Crawford's extensive range of work over a period including his years as a member of RHT and his years since then as a vocal coach, teacher and director. Many of these exercises have been experienced from inside the workshop by Bernadette Sweeney as a workshop participant, working with Kevin and other members of RHT as workshop leaders at various times. We strive here to give you the reader some tools from RHT's practice to take into your own studio, or your solo practice. Some exercises are included later which are variations of the work undertaken by the RHT under the guidance of Roy Hart and other company members. Some of these are advanced practice for the more experienced participant. Our final offerings include some exercises from other members of the original RHT and associates who now work as teachers and practitioners internationally, disseminating these practices across the world. We have undertaken this shared task to bring the work of Roy Hart and Roy Hart Theatre to the Routledge Performance Practitioners series, and to readers and users who might not otherwise have the opportunity to experience this kind of work. We encourage interested students to consider training live either at the Roy Hart Centre in Malérargues or with the many voice practitioners now working worldwide who were company members and/or have trained in these practices.

WAKING UP THE VOICE

Kevin's note: *These exercises are designed as guidelines and are not to be followed 'religiously'. The voice is a living growing organism, reflecting and indeed predisposing your general psychic and physical state of being; every individual is different and their needs are different: the context within which you are warming-up is different. Sometimes it is for a voice or drama class, it may be for very specific role or performance needs. It may be for home study. It may be more directed towards singing than text work. The space where you warm up must be taken into account. Above all, your warm-up must be relevant to you NOW. You must know not only the 'bones' of the exercise but more importantly 'Why?'. In the long run this will prove more beneficial and will enable you to invent or reinvent your own variations. Listening and vocalising are twin activities; each one leading the other on: but beware the listening becoming too 'intellectual'. Listen with all your body: vocalise without censoring...*

4.1 TO BEGIN

Situation: Lying on floor; long spine in full contact with ground: knees bent, flat of the feet firmly on the floor, legs parallel, shoulder-width apart. Breathe in with no sound either through nose or mouth: feel the air enter without force or snatching, calmly like inhaling a fragrance, no hurry. The air caresses the corridors of the sinuses, mouth, pharynx, neck and trachea, like a long tube down to the centre of the body, just below the belly button.

With your hand feel the natural unforced swell of the navel on the in-breath. Feel also the flanks expanding and the lower back spreading out on the floor as you BREATHE IN – hold for a tiny suspension – then BREATHE OUT: no force, feel how the air is gently expelled from the middle navel and flank and small of the back region.

When you have reached the end of the out-breath, like the end of a wave, there is a momentary suspension and, without willing it, your navel and flanks open out again to make way for the fragrant air that is filling you up.

Side coaching: *DO NOTHING in this exercise: relax and 'let it happen', don't make it happen or force an unnatural expansion through tightening the abdominal wall. Let it come from inside: let it start small: gradually your body will come to recognise that it can breathe 'deeply' without forcing. The upper* *chest is tranquil; this does not mean it may not move, particularly at the end of the in-breath, but it is not the prime-mover: it fulfils a secondary role once the correct impulse for the breathing is found. At no time should the shoulders tense or be lifted up or forward. You can help yourself by 'imagining' that you are melting into the floor: that the breath itself has weight and that it is dropping. Feel how the lower back can fall into the floor: no resistance.*

4.2 STRETCHING THE BREATH

This exercise can be combined with the use of numbers to augment the DURATION of breath both on the in- and out-breath. Count (at first silently), beginning with five counts for the in-breath, five on suspension and five on the out-breath, short beat before following in-breath. There should be no sound at all and no tension in the neck and tongue region. Gradually you can increase the count: try increasing the out-breath by more counts than the in-breath – the suspension between in and out should remain on 5. So:

    in-breath 5
    suspend 5
    out-breath 5
    beat
    in-breath 5
    suspend 5
    out-breath 6
    beat
    in-breath 5
    suspend 5
    out-breath 8
    beat
    and so on till you reach 10 or even 15

Once you have mastered the silent count, move to an SSSSS, then a SHHHHHHH, sound on the out-breaths. Then proceed to speak numbers out loud on a light but not breathy sound, building up to a firmer sound with a full tone. You can continue to increase the count but do not go beyond the point where the abdominal muscles contract strongly: the emphasis should be on smooth and sustained numbers without undue tension in face, jaw, lips, throat and abdominal and intercostal muscles.

Note: If in these exercises you feel constricted at the back of the neck it may be because your head is not sitting in line with your upper vertebrae; the use of a small book placed underneath your head can correct this.

BREATH, BONE, MUSCLE, SOUND

*Kevin's note: This series of exercises is much influenced by Dominique Dupuy, dancer, choreography and 'grand pedagogue' whose teaching was seminal for many members of the company over a ten-year period stretching from the late seventies. Dominique Dupuy is a figure of reference for modern dance in France, his teaching a personal synthesis that combines the pioneering work of Martha Graham, Hanya Holm and Mary Wigman, with his experience in the **Pilates** and the **Feldenkrais** approaches to the body.*

The Pilates system, named after its founder Joseph Pilates, has become a well-recognised system for exercising the human body and for rehabilitation following injury or ill-use.

The Feldenkrais method takes its name from Moshé Pinchas Feldenkrais, its originator, whose research led him to conceive a series of slow, gentle movements that allow the practitioner to become more aware of neuromuscular patterns in order to enhance functioning.

This series energises breath, activates elasticity and reflex in the rib / lung / diaphragm / viscera and develops synergy between deep muscular systems, skeletal vibration and diaphragmatic tonicity, thus giving a sense of foundation or 'support' to the sound.

4.3 THE PELVIC CLOCK

Situation: Lie down on the floor with your back at right angles to the wall and your toes against the wall (you may wish to place a yoga mat underneath your spine and pelvis): the knees are raised and pointed to the ceiling – keep your heels on the floor, while the toes and ball of the foot should be pressed firmly against the wall, arms resting comfortably on the floor, palms facing up (see Figure 4.1.).

Figure 4.1 Exercise 4.3: The Pelvic Clock with actor Aimee Paxton, image by Bernadette Sweeney.

Bring your attention to your pelvis: without moving yet, make a mental journey starting at your tail bone, the small knobbly bone at the base of your spinal column – let your attention travel up from the tail bone to the triangle of the sacrum, a series of five bones that are fused together in the adult body – and then continue your inner journey up to the five lumbar vertebrae, which articulate with each other and with the thoracic vertebrae above and the fused sacrum below. *Visualise* a clock that is lying with its clock face looking up towards the ceiling at the level of this necklace of vertebrae that stretches from the tail bone to the topmost lumbar vertebrae. Midday on this clock corresponds to this topmost lumbar area and six o'clock is the tail bone.

Start gently rolling along your spine from six o'clock (the tail bone) to midday (the top lumbar). You will be tracing a straight line on the floor. Don't raise the pelvis off the floor. You will probably notice that as you roll back towards six o'clock, a part of your sacrum and lumbar vertebrae lift off the ground creating a bridge. As you roll to midday, these vertebrae will tend to drop and flatten towards the floor. The amount of rise and fall of this part of the spine varies a lot given each individual's morphology. Don't overemphasise, simply follow your pathway on the floor as you roll from six o'clock to midday and back, and let the rising and falling of the vertebrae be a result of that motion.

Now gradually let the breath accompany you. Let the in-breath drop in as you roll towards six o'clock, let it release out as you roll back to midday. Feel that breath and movement are one. Gradually involve the feet in an active way. The heels remain on the floor. Press with the toes and the ball of the foot against the wall on the out-breath, as you release and roll back towards midday. It should feel like you are ringing a doorbell with the toes and ball of the foot. Firm, sustained but precise. Imagine that it is this action of the toes and ball of the foot against the wall that is expelling the air outwards, channelling it up through the legs and pelvis, until it sweeps through your sacrum and lumbar regions as it travels up and out your body through mouth and nose. Release the pressure of the toes and ball of the foot on the in-breath as you roll to six o'clock. Reapply it as you once again release the breath and roll back to midday.

Kevin's note: *The aim of this journey is to find fluidity and connection between feet, pelvis, spine and the breath. We are looking for a sense of melting on the out-breath and of effortless filling up on the in-breath. Don't think of contracting surface abdominal muscles on the out-breath, rather think of the out-breath starting in your feet, travelling through the back of your pelvis, and continuing its journey up along the spine through the neck to the head.*

Now ... transform the silent breath to an SSS ... then a SHHH and finally to a soft sigh as you build up a rhythm to the movement of the pelvis without losing the action of the feet on the sound. Release your pressure with heels or toes on the in-breath. Gradually you increase the amplitude of the movement and let the sigh gain in strength.

Once you have a firm sound you can experiment: let the sigh become more of a siren or glissando sound, sometimes from high to low, sometimes low to high. Then alternate tapped sounds HUH-HUH-HUH followed by one long held note, all on one out-breath.

Side Coaching: *Melt into floor; breath, sound and movement are all one; drop sound into floor; release jaw and open up back of mouth and soft palate area; soften shoulders. Use all the time of the breath for the movement: movement and breath are one. Feel how your sound is born from the navel: feel how the mouth remains relaxed,* *tongue relaxed, with a sensation of openness in the area of the larynx. Experiment with different notes. Be aware how the rolling motion of the pelvis resonates all the way up the spinal column gradually inducing a slight nodding motion in the head.*

4.4 SACRA-LUMBAR STRETCH

Situation: Lying on floor on your back (with a yoga mat underneath pelvis, spine and head, if you wish for extra comfort). Place the feet with the soles flat on the floor: your knees are perpendicular to the floor and pointed towards the ceiling; now raise pelvis 10–15cm off the floor (you can test this by placing a fist under your pelvis, it should fit snugly in the space between pelvis and floor), arms resting comfortably on the floor, palms facing up (see Figure 4.2).

Imagine that there is a necklace of pearls leading from the tail bone in the air to the lower thoracic vertebrae (just above the lumbar region, that you engaged in the previous exercise) that are on the ground – your tail bone and sacra-lumbar regions are suspended in the air. Make sure

Figure 4.2 Exercise 4.4: Sacra-Lumbar Stretch, with actor Aimee Paxton, image by Bernadette Sweeney.

Figure 4.3 Exercise 4.4: Sacra-Lumbar Stretch: Variation 1, with actor Aimee Paxton, image by Bernadette Sweeney.

your buttocks are not clenched – your pelvis is maintained in place by the action of the feet into the floor: let your breath settle into the navel region. *Imagine* that the necklace of vertebrae between the tail bone and this lower thoracic zone is melting: that every vertebra is hanging off its neighbours. As you breathe out, *imagine* that your breath too is heavy and that it is falling towards the spinal column; all the internal organs are dropping.

Now, release very progressively to the floor with successive out-breaths sighing abundantly, as you focus your sound on to the vertebral body that is sinking into floor. Take four or five out-breaths progressing from the lower thoracic area to lumbar to sacrum and finally to the tail bone.

Side coaching*: In this exercise the accent is on sensing how your whole respiratory apparatus is grounded in the lower part of the body; we are not looking for a 'pure' sound, and there will not be long held sounds: rather the sound will be breathy, very sighed and with a sensation of depth in the note and humidity and warmth in the texture. Concentrate on achieving the maximum inner connection between breath,* *sound, navel and lower spine: accent is on the out-breath. Once a vertebra is on the ground don't bring it up again. Learn to isolate area by area, vertebra by vertebra. This is important for really defining your inner vocal territory!*

Variation 1: Lying on floor on your back (with a yoga mat underneath pelvis, spine and head, if you wish for extra comfort): place the feet with the soles flat on the floor: your knees are perpendicular to the floor and pointed towards the ceiling. Visualise your central body divided into four segments – sternum and collarbone; central ribs (the branch of ribs that radiates around your central body below the base of the sternum); waistline (below the line of the ribs and above your pelvis); and pubis/sacrum (corresponds to the lowest spinal vertebrae).

Now, push into the floor with your feet and raise the entire length of your spinal column off the floor with the pelvis suspended in the air while the top of your shoulders stay on the ground, arms resting comfortably on the floor, palms facing up (see Figure 4.3.)

As you breath in *imagine* breath flows in only to the sternum and collarbone area. Let that area of your body swell with the in-breath, then, on a sighed out-breath, let the sternum and collarbone drop to the floor.

The second in-breath fills and swells the central rib area, then drop this area to the floor on the sighed out-breath.

The third in-breath is directed towards waist area, which is then released to the floor on sighed out-breath three. In-breath four is directed to pubis/sacrum area, and on sighed out-breath four this area is then released to the floor.

Side coaching: *Keep tail bone up as far as possible till the end (i.e. let it down very progressively so spinal column is stretched). Try and sigh out through the part of bone structure that is about to drop to the floor. Find a vocal balance between actively letting go and passively dropping weight: ensure mouth is open and that air passage and throat sensation is open and not scratchy or rough – find the weight of the breath. See what happens to the sound: are you led to change the notes? Do you want to slide them? Be careful not to raise off the ground any segment that has already released into the floor. Use gravity, use the feeling of dropping and letting go; this is not a 'placing' exercise, rather it is a feeling of giving up ... However, you have to be quite precise in maintaining the isolation in the different areas; otherwise the effect is lost ...*

Variation 2: You can then complete this exercise series by performing the descent in one long sighing sound (as in a siren), making sure you observe the progressive nature of the release into the floor; let your sound go with the falling into the floor: don't hold on. In general, in this series of exercises use an open-mouthed sigh on an AH (as in father). When you get used to it though, you can experiment with different vowels particularly I (as in pie), O (as in low), OW (as in cow), WHO (as in who).

Variation 3: Once you have completed the siren sound (probably on a descent), speak some words with the low open sound you have reached. Try sitting up now and maintaining the same vocal 'place' continue to speak with this open-throated low resonant sound. If you don't have any text immediately available to you simply speak the word 'Holiness'. Try now to change the pitch but keep the same sensation in your mouth, jaw and throat. Can you keep the link to your pelvis and lower belly? Is there resonance and feeling in the ribs?

Side coaching: Beware of forcing the movement or the sound: the key is to release the body weight in the given area, and let the sound also release. You can work this exercise in partners, assisting each other by gentle pressure of the hands to achieve the sensation of 'dropping' into the floor. Look for the PELVIC CAVE SOUNDS – dark, low sound area that seems to engage the viscera and pelvic area, stimulating a sense of vibration in the sacrum zone.

4.5 STANDING VARIATIONS OF THE PELVIC CLOCK

This exercise uses pressure against a wall or a partner to stimulate a sense of vibration and resonance in the sacrolumbar region. This pressure encourages the engagement of the transverse abdominal muscle, that underpins your voice in this area!

Situation: Position yourself standing with your back against a wall, feet approximately at shoulder-width apart, parallel, and fully planted on the floor, roughly your own foot length from wall. Place sacra-lumbar area against wall, but do not touch with any other area of the spine or back: this is an isolation exercise (see Figure 4.4.). This time The Pelvic Clock is on the wall at the level of your sacra-lumbar region looking directly towards the wall in front of you. Six o'clock is still your tail bone and midday your uppermost lumbar vertebra. This time the flat of the foot is on the floor. Breath in, rolling sacra-lumbar region on wall till you reach six o'clock (tail bone). As you breath out, press (as if you press a doorbell) actively into the floor with the whole foot, and, using that sustained pressure as the impulse for the movement, roll back

Figure 4.4 Exercise 4.5: Standing Variations of The Pelvic Clock, with actor Aimee Paxton, image by Bernadette Sweeney.

along the wall on the sacra-lumbar vertebrae towards midday (uppermost lumbar vertebra) as you sing out.

Variation 1: Find PELVIC CAVE SOUND again and gradually transform this sound into a sustained held note on a 'CLEAR' sound (low pitch area) on AH (father) or OH (woe) or AW (flaw).

Side coaching*: Use all the time of the breath to complete the movement. That way you can soften the lower abdomen on in-breath and start the sound from a* *slight contraction in that area, that engages the lower pelvis and links the contact of bone, wall and deep muscle tissue. Enjoy the sensation of support that the wall gives you. Remember that feeling. You can try this on different notes: see how you can sustain the sound without forcing from the tummy but with a sense of stretching your spine as you sing the breath out. Ensure that you work only on the pelvis and lower back region. The middle and upper back should not touch the wall at this point: the knees are slightly bent throughout.*

Variation 2: Commence to roll up the spinal column on the wall, starting from the sacrum, rolling up through the lumbar and up eventually to the very top of your shoulders, at the base of the neck. As you roll up make a siren sound starting from a low pitch and moving up eventually to higher pitch areas that ring in your head. You can extend this movement following through to the point where your back finally completely disengages from the wall and you are left with only your cranium pressed against the wall and your back arched. Vocally you can either:

(a) On one long out-breath, sing a siren from a low to a comfortable high pitch as you roll up the spinal column.
(b) Break this undulation down into smaller sections – tail bone to sacrum – sacrum to lumbar – lumbar to mid-spine – mid-spine till the shoulders – finally arch up from the shoulders until you place the back of the head on the wall. Let the sound gradually ascend from a low pitch to a high one taking a new in-breath for each section.
(c) Once you feel confident in this variation you can also come down progressively from the top of the shoulders or the back of the head, until the entire spine makes contact with the wall progressively, the sound now gradually spiralling downwards in pitch.
(d) You can also now use FLUTTERING sounds instead of a clear one. The fluttering should be light but firm, look for smoothness and agility as you move up and down in pitch, breathe often.

Side coaching: *Take your time: try to make the in-breath part of exercise. Pick up the new sound where you left off the previous one, if you are doing the movement and sound incrementally. Slide slowly physically and vocally so you are able to 'fill in the gaps' and not leave blank spaces in your voice or in your pressure on the wall. The wall is your partner. Beware of snapping the head back if you go till the end of the movement and only the back of head is in contact with wall. Neck should not be overarched but keep link between head and chest. Remember to always start with contact established only between wall and tail* *bone, as you gradually roll up through midday (upper lumbar) until each vertebral area in turn first presses, then leaves the wall support.*

4.6 THREE HUMS: WAKING UP RESONANCE IN THE HEAD

The three hums are: M (closed lips), N (blade of tongue closes off air through mouth by pressing against walls of mouth behind upper front teeth and molars) and 'NG (like the ending of the word 'king' – the back of tongue is blocking the air passage to mouth by pressing against soft palate).

Note: *All air passes through nose, no air through your mouth. It is good to vary all three of these as each favours a particular zone: M' is general, N is frontal, NG is spinal, although you can also influence the resonance voluntarily.*

Start standing, humming freely on an MMM, explore the sound, feels its vibration around the lips, teeth, spreading into the face and skull. Same experience on NNNN, this time being aware of the bones in your sinus area, eye sockets, temples. Then hum on the NG, this time being aware of vibration in the neck vertebrae and occipital lobe.

Now you can hum, sliding up and down your voice on each of these three hums. See if you can make circles with the sound coming back to your point of departure. Then hold just one note and alternate soft and loud.

Side coaching: *Try to make these glissandi as smooth as possible: I sometimes use the French word 'onctueux', to describe this, meaning creamy like a thick yoghurt! Explore your limits. Can you keep that smooth sensation all the time or is there a point in your voice where it jumps or shifts very noticeably? Alternate the three hums so you build up a global feel of resonance in your face, head, skull and neck. Don't lose the sense of connectedness through your feet that you have built up in the previous sections. Continue to feel the 'rootedness' of the breath in the body, the impulse for the sound always coming from the navel area with a sense of activation coming up from the feet and traversing the pelvic floor. Make these glissandi as circular as possible. Don't think of high notes and low notes, but of a circle where high and low are linked and have no more importance than any of the intermediate notes.*

Variation 1: *Glissandi –* as you start on your base note, slide one foot sideways and reach out with arms to side and then out. The knees bend low and as you hit highest note you are a in low *plié* with arms outstretched to sides at shoulder level – *the vertical motion of the glissando* *is contrasted with the horizontal motion of the body so you 'think' more of widening and less of narrowing as pitch rises.*

As you drop in pitch to return to base note, finish movement so arms arrive at ear height stretched to the ceiling and legs slowly straighten out of plié. As pitch drops your body and arms accentuate an upwards arc, contrasting the dropping pitch, so you don't 'collapse' on to the lower pitches

Variation 2: Once you have mastered this movement, change direction on each new vocalisation so you get the sense of space and width throughout the studio. Imagine the four directions – forward, back, up, down – and let your glissando reach out into each of these directions in turn.

Variation 3: Jump from one hum to another in slow or quick succession as you freely change pitch. Note different sensations of resonance in face, neck, cranium, chest. If you flick quickly from one to the other, it may sound like African Xhosa – a Bantu language with an abundant use of click consonants.

Transition

Link a fullness of resonance in a hummed sound to an open sound through a transitionary phase. You can do this with each of the three hums we have explored so far:

(a) Letting jaw drop and opening mouth slightly on M
(b) By peeling blade of the tongue slightly away on N
(c) By peeling back of the tongue slightly away on NG

Side coaching: *Ensure that the sound retains the harmonic richness of the hum! Engage the breath and the ribs and an abdominal sense of support. Retain the 'buzz' of the hummed sound while you let some of the air pass through the mouth. NOTHING CHANGES. The sound remains vibrant and 'wide', 'diffuse'. Use the soft palate to help open up on the higher notes, but don't open the mouth too wide. Commence sound in the hum for a moment, ensuring hum is solid, then drop jaw or tongue slightly for half-open sound: think of a very French EN or ON sound ('en suite' or 'mon oncle'. Your inner sensation should be that there is no or very little difference between the hum and the transitional sound.*

4.7 PROGRESS TO FULL SOUND

Amplify and conduct resonance to a fully sung or spoken sound. Complete the arc from hum to fully sung sound. Now you can develop to full sound but again DON'T INVENT ANYTHING; if your preparation is correct just let it happen:

(a) Starting with the M hum, progress through the transitional sound to a fully open sound on OOH (as in moo ...) by simply dropping your jaw and allowing the sound to ripple forward from the hum: top of the neck is soft, not tense.
(b) Starting with the N hum, progress through the transitional sound to a fully open sound on EE (as in knee) by releasing tongue from its place on ridge behind front teeth and molars and allowing mouth to open fully: head poised not stiff.
(c) Starting with the NG hum, progress through transitional sound to a fully open sound on ah (as in laugh). Feel the soft palette lift off from the tongue which peels away, as the mouth opens fully: neck remains fluid and may make micro-movements as it adjusts.

Side coaching: *Propel the sound forward, retain the harmonic wholeness of the hum and let it be taken forward and out of you, as if the sound were a cascade of gold flowing from your lips*

4.8 VOCAL PLAYFULNESS

Now you are 'warmed up', start playing more vocally: there are several avenues for this. 'Runs' (*glissandi*): starting from a low pitch on an open AH (father) or OH (holiness), let your voice slide up progressively without forcing to a high note (at this point you can decide to take another in-breath or not), then descend to the low note where you began. This can be a long journey punctuated with several breaths ... Try to maintain a sense of lightness in this and width in the voice, especially as you move up into the higher registers, ideally you want these transitions to be smooth, without bumps. Activate sternum and spinal column (through undulations) in order to maintain connectedness between low register (pelvis) and high register (head/neck). This exercise can be even further developed by taking more time with it, so it becomes a real vocal journey through your own vocal landscape, teasing out timbre, volume, colour and emotional imagery.

Side coaching: *Don't forget to breathe, let the in-breath be part of the vocal world, release belly on in-breath, IN-Spire. You can use the contact with the wall or undulating against a partner to help!*

Variation – 'Fluttering': Similar exercise to above but with the voice fluttering, a rapid but not forced vibration that comes from the vocal folds: the air pressure remains constant. Look for agility as you slide up and down, note unusual qualities or even characters that surface: stay with them, develop them and then continue the fluttering slides. Vary vowels and note how each vowel change affects vocal quality and the very shape and effort in the mouth and vocal tract! From the 'fluttering' exercise every so often land on a note and hold it so you will alternate fluttering slides and held note: you can relate this to the space around you and vary dynamics, volume and intention.

4.9 MOVING TOWARDS THE SPEAKING VOICE

(a) Imagine you are about to throw a javelin. Take a step back and recoil as you prepare the throw, breathe in, start an energetic hum (either MMM, NNNN or NG) and as you explode forward balancing weight on to the front leg, hurl the javelin, at the same instant releasing the hum into a fully open sound with the javelin: follow the imaginary javelin with your sound in a long, long arc until it hits its Olympic target hundreds of metres away.

Side coaching*: although this throw engages a rush of kinetic energy don't let it unbalance you: keep the centre of gravity low and follow the javelin with your gesture as it flashes through the air: remember your sound is an action, not a position, so body too is fully mobilized but not locked.*

(b) Starting from a very buzzing Z sound build up an explosive Zee (as in 'zeal'). Begin it on the edge of a whisper, building it up on different pitches, making sure the sound is well resonated in the head and chest. Throw the sound away from you, using gestures.

The following four progressions (c–f) of 4.9 aim to connect the actions of the mouth, jaw, tongue and palette with the breath and diaphragmatic resilience, whilst being aware of how these sounds resonate throughout the whole body and head. As we start to generate short units of verbal sound, gradually stretching these isolated building blocks of sound into full words, lines of text and finally an entire text reveals itself. By accentuating the energy, the muscular energy of resistance and release, that jaw, tongue and lip enact with the flexible spatial configuration of mouth and windpipe, we invite the whole body, from chest through ribs, from neck down the spine to pelvis and even the feet, to take part in that exploration and give it a sense of support and embodiment.

(c) Explore consonants: moving back from lips (P, B) to tongue against ridge behind front teeth (T, D), to back of tongue against soft palette (K, G): sense the change from the unvoiced first consonant of each pair(for example P) to the second voiced consonant (for example B) in each pair. Play with dynamics: variation in pressure and force of articulation; extend consonant into a vowel sound, experiment with pitch, volume, direction, intention of sound.

(d) Long vowel sounds; find words with diphthongs or triphthongs, 'lawn', 'weight', 'flown', 'round', 'stay', 'joint', et cetera. Make up your own words with expanded open vowel sounds. Explore the articulation of the vowel and how the consonant leads into the vowel and vice versa.

(e) Take a line of text you are currently working on. Explore individually all the consonant-vowel connections, feel the muscularity of the words. Vary dynamics and timing. Teach your version to someone else: learn their words and their versions. Find body movement to mirror the muscular sense of the words. Build up to the whole phrase making sure you are equally present vocally throughout. Vary pitch and dynamics. Pass them round one to another so you learn many different 'bites' of sound.

(f) Go now to a whole speech that you are working on. Speak it in a devoiced whisper, concentrating on really articulating the words and letting the sense saturate you. Gradually come 'on to your voice' increasing volume, retaining the rhythm and the concentration on the sense. Let your voice discover the interpretation through the rhythm, force and drive of the words. It may surprise you.

4.10 VIOLIN, VIOLA, CELLO

Kevin's note: *This exercise brings together two important strands in the Roy Hart Tradition: the extension of the range in each register and the ability to expand the quality and timbre over a very restricted range. It also often makes use of images and characters to engage the student and give a firm reference for a diversity of vocal qualities. The exercise pivots around three fundamental voices or qualities represented by three stringed instruments: the cello, viola and violin. Sometimes, depending on the teacher, a fourth instrumental quality is added: the double bass. Commonly called* Violin, Viola, Cello, *this exercise enables the student to identify different zones of resonance and engagement in the body, and serves as an entry point into an exploration of an infinity of vocal colours. The metaphor of violin, viola, cello allows participants to open up three main centres for vocal engagement and sensation: the pelvis and legs (cello), the* *heart and sternum (viola), the face, head, cranium (violin). Finally, it is a very useful jumping-off point for further exploration in singing and text-based work, stimulating fresh perspectives for the performer.* Violin, Viola, Cello *appears in the teaching of many practitioners influenced either directly or indirectly by Roy Hart, and has been moulded to suit their style and context. It is certainly one of the 'oldest' teaching tools in this tradition as Wolfsohn used it extensively and his pupils in the 1950s made some very impressive recordings using these word cues.*

The version below is drawn from recent practice by Kevin Crawford and assumes that this takes place with a small group although it is also possible to experience this sequence alone. Although we are able to be very clear about changes in pitch or volume in a person's sound, and these changes can be described with relative accuracy, it is sometimes harder to find the appropriate words for the changes in sound in this exercise: the ability to hold on to vocal colour despite pitch change. To describe this therefore we tend to use three words interchangeably: quality, colour and timbre.

Pitch indications: We have referenced notes from the piano that will probably suit lower voices. Higher voices may sing one octave above my indications where they are more comfortable. The facilitator/leader may adapt these indications to suit the participants' needs.

Sounding the cello: Pelvis and legs

First, without piano or indication of notes, imagine deep belly laughter bubbling up; then mime this extravagantly, holding on to big 'Falstaff-size' bellies. Slowly let this deep chasmic laugh become audible: face one another – let it be contagious – feel the engagement below the waistline, the feet may drum the floor – the legs can open out into a wide position, knees bent as if the pelvis is opening to the floor – the pelvis becomes heavier and hangs down to the earth. Activate the base of the pelvis and sacrum area by making scooping and digging movements with the tail bone. Let this deep bubbling laugh rock you for a moment and let yourself be supported by cavernous laughter from around you. Gradually let the laugh subside but keep hold of this deep, dark place in your voice. At this point either a participant or ideally a facilitator/leader will play a low note on the piano (an octave below middle C). Let your laugh sound extend into a held note on an open vowel, AHH or OHH as you follow the piano. If you are working with a workshop leader, they might allow the solos to unfold in the following way, otherwise work on this for yourself in solo practice. Gradually you will go semitone by semitone up to higher pitches, but you need to hold on to the colour and quality of the sound that you had on the low notes. Once the leader feels you are beginning to lose the quality of the sound, they will bring you back down again to the lower notes where you find it more easily and instinctively. This journey can be repeated several times until you are satisfied you can extend the low dark deep quality upwards over say an octave. At this point the word *cello* can be introduced, always with that dark colour engaging pelvis and lower body. Take the stance of an imaginary standing cellist, feeling the deep reverberations of the cello as you draw your imaginary bow across the strings. Try to imagine the radiating mellifluous cello pouring out into your sound. Again, you can repeat several times the journey from a very low note to roughly an octave higher with the aim of maintaining a consistent colouring to the sound. Notice how the two vowels in *cello* might each affect the sound quality. Can you keep them consistent or does the quality change according to the vowel? Take a moment to shake out and let *cello* go ... absorb what you have experienced.

Sounding the violin: Head, face, cranium

Now let your attention spiral up to your face and head. Feel your whole body become light and airy. Maybe a smile plays on your lips. Let a soft sigh slide out of you as sway slightly with this light-headedness. Your lower body now is less earthbound, more balletic in quality. Still without a piano to guide you, let the sighs become more drawn out until they are long notes, light and ethereal. Feel the sound rising into your cranial cavity and maybe even beyond as it follows its ascension out through the top of your head. Are there open sounds that seem to help you more to find that stellar quality? Our pianist leads you into a specific note around middle C, and you follow the piano up and down keeping that light and suspended quality. Try experimenting with an EEE (me ...) or an IH (Mi ... key Mouse) sound. At this point the word *violin* is introduced. Imagine yourself holding the violin, a much smaller bodied instrument than the cello – its sound is less corporeal, it seems to reach upward beyond the pull of gravity. Mime holding the violin, chin slightly tucked under and singing as you bow. The leader again takes you on a journey, this time downwards in pitch, to the point where you lose the light timbre and can no longer sustain the quality. Try and keep the same quality on all the vowel sounds, noting where it is easier. Each time you make the journey try to keep the colour consistent. Clearly this is not always possible but you may be surprised how long you can go and still be tethered to that silky-fine violin quality. Take a rest, how does your body feel now. Can you remember what it felt like to produce those violin-like sounds?

Sounding the viola: Heart and sternum

Start by gently advancing and retreating with the sternum, your breastbone. Feel how it can stretch forward, pointing away from your ribs or retreat into the chest cavity leading the vertebra to extend backwards. As you do this let the breath flow in this area, irrigating your heart and upper chest area. The breath should feel wide and slightly yawned, as if you are making space at the back of your mouth cavity, widening and stretching the laryngeal zone. The centre of your body is now the sternum/heart area: the breath becomes thicker and sound starts to emanate. It is slightly hollow, reverberating in your sternum, between the rich thickness of the lower body cello quality and the thinner needle of the violin head timbre. It is in some sense a 'mixed' sound partaking of both these timbres but still with a clear signature quality of its own. What open sounds favour this tone? Is it easier on an OH (mow) or an OOH (through) sound? Where do you find this sound in your voice? Can you slide up and down on it? Can you pass the sound around between you and hear how each person is finding their version? The pianist begins to play a note, middle C and takes the group up and down. You may find you can hold this sound better in notes above middle C, or below. Notice when you can't. Now include the *viola*. Take hold of the viola. It is bigger than the violin but smaller than the cello. Its body has a fuller tone than the violin but lacks the bass amplitude of the cello. As you play it, imagine its vibrations penetrate the chest and fill out the sound. Notice which open sounds on the word *viola* favour this mixed quality. Continue to engage the sternum as you sing.

Take a rest now and re-map in your mind's eye the three timbres/instruments/ physical centres that we have explored so far.

Linking

The next step is to link the three 'instruments'. At this point the leader of the session (or yourself if you are alone) might want to offer difference in range for lower and higher voices. Kevin Crawford has observed that the notes around middle C suit some higher voices better: similarly, the notes around the G below middle C suit some lower voices better. But these are only approximations and can vary immensely from one voice to another. Choose therefore a note that is in the centre of your range. This will be the point of departure. Now alternate the three colours using the words *cello, viola, violin* – *in that order* – taking care to maintain the colour for each 'instrument' that you found previously: keep the mime of the instrument and the bodily focus for each timbre. Try this first allowing one full out-breath for reach instrument. Now, see if you can link all three instruments in one full breath. This will certainly be more challenging. At this point you may wish to let go miming the instrument and instead use the body fully to bring out character and colour. Gradually start working up and down over a range of several semitones from the starting note and see if you can hold these qualities. As you go up in pitch it will become harder to maintain the dark timbre of cello, as you go down the violin quality may weaken. Similarly, viola may be fuller on certain notes. This sequence works best if all participants sustain a physical and vocal mime as each person sings in turn.

You are now ready to bring even more vitality and bounce to the three qualities by introducing characters and further timbre variations. Try using the following words for each of the three qualities

Violin now becomes: 'I am the little Princess'
Viola now becomes: 'I am the Queen'
Cello now becomes: 'I am the King'

Once again repeat the sequence using these words whilst developing each character: the King might have a big gut and heavy boots; the Queen is regal and full chested; the Princess is light, solar

Variation 1: Richard Armstrong often worked with other archetypes: the violin as an elf, the viola as a diva, the cello as a duchess. He would then introduce a fourth character and quality, the double bass, as a variety of spontaneously invented characters, one being simply being based on the shape and form of the instrument itself. In his version the four zones would effectively divide the height and depth of resonance into four, leading to partner conducting the shifts on a single pitch. After later taking away the character divisions, the conducting would lead to free-form shifts of resonance throughout the whole body, initially on a single tone, and eventually with conducting of height and depth of pitch and resonance, with the conducting partners using one hand for resonance, the other for pitch.

Variation 2: Kevin Crawford also adds another variation: using a very nasal pointed witch-like sound participants sing on one note: 'I am the wicked witch of the west'. This is sung at the end of the sequence after 'I am the little Princess' and comes as contrast to the more angelic, heady princess sound. These variations can also be performed over a small compass of your range, and will bring increased nuance and flexibility to the middle of your range.

Application to singing and text-work

This exercise can be very useful when applied to text and song work: for instance you can try to speak/sing your text with only one of these four timbres, sticking though to one note throughout. The sheer reduction in range and timbre may bring out an aspect of the text that you had not noticed. Or you may ask a partner to 'conduct' you as you speak/sing your text on one note. The partner indicates to you where the sound is located in your body, thus directing you to vary your vocal quality. Once again this may unstick you from your habitual textual path and refresh your contact with the words. The same principle can be applied to a song although in this case there will be melodic variation. However, you may wish to maintain the same quality throughout a phrase or be directed to vary greatly your timbre by your partner. There is a wide range of games that can be played using the form of this exercise either alone, in partner or in group. Through *Violin, Viola, Cello*, we open up a palette of vocal colours and a control of nuance in our middle range. Combined with *Exploring Height and Depth*, it covers both the horizontal and the vertical parameters in the human voice.

KEVIN CRAWFORD'S MALÉRARGUES WORKSHOP – SUMMER 2019

These exercises are designed for a group of performers who wish to discover new facets and performance possibilities by working with a piece of spoken text. Participants will need to wear comfortable clothes that they can move in and work in bare feet or soft shoes. They will need to have memorised a substantial monologue which they will rework during the workshop in a number of ways. Ideally this exploration should be led by a teacher, or by a more experienced member of the ensemble.

4.11 WAKING UP CENTRES OF RESONANCE WITH A SHORT TEXT

This section uses three main centres of resonance and energy: the base of the sternum, the false ribs and the lower abdominal zone are activated using the following words:

> *Love-Love-Lover*
> *Gold-Gold-Golden*
> *Golden Lover*

As you explore this sequence keep a feeling of bouncy energy: don't sit on the words but lift them up. There are no fixed pitches: let your voice find its own level for each centre of resonance/energy.

Workshop leader or assigned participant will lead the following in call-and-response: (a) Place hands on lower sternum and speak *Love-Love-Lover* breathing in with a slight beat between each word. Speak with firm sound but not loud at first, feeling the vibration in your sternum beneath your hand, and the sound radiating out through your ribcage from that point.

Note: *Release any contraction in abdomen as you breath in.*

Repeat the sequence three times.

Workshop leader or assigned participant will lead the following in call-and-response: (b) Descend hands so fingers curl around the false ribs (ribs 8–10) that you find by feeling the rib bones that delimit the edge of your abdominal wall from your ribcage at the front of your chest. Your thumb meanwhile presses slightly lower on your back once again finding the lowest rib curve it can touch. This corresponds to your so-called lowest floating ribs (numbers 11 and 12) (see Figure 4.5).

Feel the expansion of these lower ribs as you breath in and their contraction towards the centre of the body as you breathe out.

Now repeat *Love-Love-Lover*, this time directing the focus of the sound to these ribs and feeling both some vibration in the ribs and the engagement of muscles just below them. The sound becomes a little darker, rounder. Start not loud, but firm and with a fuller tone.

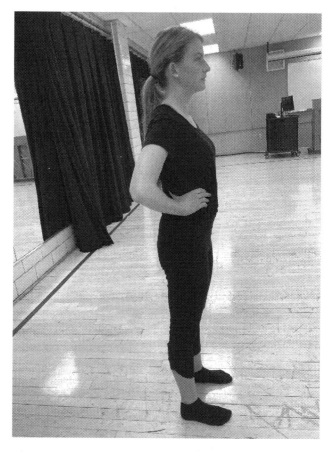

Figure 4.5 Exercise 4.11 Waking Up Centres of Resonance with a Short Text, with actor Aimee Paxton, image by Bernadette Sweeney.

Workshop leader or assigned participant will lead the following in call-and-response: (c) Now place your hands, one on top of the other on a space a finger's width down from your belly button. You are now going to focus your energy and intention in this area as you speak *Love-Love-Lover*. This time you won't probably feel any vibration in this zone (no bones to conduct vibration) but you may feel the engagement of the abdominal muscles (and beneath them, the transverse muscle), that contracts on each word. You may have a feeling of pushing from this region. Try not to influence or control the push but let it happen. Be aware of the whole circumference of the lower abdomen, viscera and pelvic floor. Does your belly tend to contract or to expand slightly? Note the direction you tend to favour and try the other direction to see how it feels and whether this has an effect on the words. Now your quality is probably even darker in colour, with a strong feeling of pelvic support. Again, start not too loud, but fully inviting the area beneath your fingers to be the source of the sound. Repeat three times *Love-Love-Lover*

(d) Repeat the whole of this sequence – (a), (b), (c) – on the words *Gold-Gold-Golden* three times

(e) Repeat the whole of this sequence on the words *Golden Lover* three times

Variation 1: Keeping a bounce and a liveliness in your body as you repeat all three texts on each level once only (sternum, ribs, abdomen). Now you can start to play more actively with each physical and vocal quality. You might like to imagine you are a seductive or impassioned lover …

Variation 2: Each student now takes a short phrase (3–5 words) from their own text and uses it as material, based on the same three body centres and qualities. Different participants may be highlighted and repeat their version using their own text which are then taken up either by an individual or the whole group. Ask participants to be more dynamic and bring the improvisation to a heightened dramatic level.

4.12 WAKING UP THE VOICE FURTHER

Now participants, using their own monologues, explore individually where their texts sit in their bodies. Taking a slow pace they expand, repeat and invest, each word first, then phrase, as they somatically scan which areas of the body and head are involved. Obviously, this is a less codified experience than the previous sequence, but is an invitation to further 'embody' the words of your text. At first you can continue to touch/search with your fingers to denote the area that is activated by the word or syllable.

4.13 LEADING TEXT WITH MOVEMENT IN PAIRS

In partners, A leads B's movement with gentle hand contact on different parts of the body, while B speaks. A applies gentle but clear pressure to a part of B's body (including head, legs, arms ...). B responds by stretching towards the point of contact with A as if they wish to reach out to that hand, or to push it away ... B starts to speak text, thinking of directing text to that point of contact, using the slight resistance from A to help to stretch towards A and to sound their text into the body area that is activated. Once A feels that B has exhausted the action of opening the body towards that particular contact point, they unhurriedly change the contact point to another area of B. A should, in listening, give B the opportunity to make slow and big contrasts in voice quality depending on the zone that is implicated. A also becomes aware of B's tendencies and invites B to explore less familiar vocal territory through the text. Once the two have established a good rhythm and creative listening, A can challenge B by making more sudden changes both in terms of speed and quality.

When you have explored for approximately 3–5 minutes, change roles. Once you have established a sensitive and clear communication between you, start to change roles more often. This is almost like a game of tag between two and can be very playful. Your touch might be just the tip of a finger, or it might be more active with the pressure of the whole hand. You can also begin to allow moments of increased physical contact. You can allow partners to lean on each other giving weight, releasing textual energy through the act of weight sharing.

Kevin's note: *The aim of this is to encourage B to move outside their habitual textual pathways and surprise them into discovering other nuances and associations in the text. At this point the more codified structure gives way to a more intuitive exploration. With this or any other movement that involves partners making physical contact with each other, make sure to talk through the exercise in advance, and consider having participants indicate where they are comfortable being touched, any old injuries that should be avoided, et cetera. Make sure to acknowledge the comfort levels within the group: for instance, have they worked together over a long period of time, or are they just newly working together? A well-established group may be able to move through these exercises and sensitivities more quickly than a newer group. In any case, ensure that participants feel safe, and free to step outside the work to observe instead at any point if they would prefer.*

Variation 1: Now continue solo but as if still feeling points of contact from your partner – imagine your partner is still touching you, giving you resistance, or you are leaning giving weight to the partner. Try to retain the feeling of partnering – you are not alone. Once you have generously explored this, expressing the text with full vocal and physical engagement, gradually reduce the scope of your movement but keep that sense of aliveness INSIDE your body. Let it inform the text, until finally you are standing addressing the others, your words, freshly hatched, emotion informing your pauses, pitch and volume.

Note: For the transition from full movement to a stripped-down physical simplicity, the workshop leader may coach you through this process.

Variation 2: As you become more at ease with exploring touch, giving and taking weight, resistance and dynamic pauses, both A and B can work with their monologues at the same time, as they continue to explore their movement duologue. Sometimes they may speak almost simultaneously, sometimes one then the other, sometimes, silence. The two monologues now are pitted against and with each other. You may find moments of great contrast, tragic or comic. Moments when A and B are tuned to the same intention, then separate and then maybe collide or splinter off.

Kevin's note: *This variation can give rise to unsuspected meanings and associations in your text, because it is now in a totally unforeseen context. Perhaps what seemed a quiet reflective moment suddenly explodes in rage, or a pain-filled scream shifts into a tender laugh as your partner makes a surprise move. Fluctuations in status between A and B also provoke new perspectives for meaning and nuance. A and B listen profoundly to each other: they listen through their bodies, they listen through the sound, they listen through the words. A patchwork of actions and reactions surfaces. The workshop leader may wish to encourage a direction the work takes or discourage an initiative. Their listening too is fundamental to the potential creativity of this variation. They should also be aware when the improvisation is reaching its end, and should let their input be guided by their knowledge of the boundaries and potential of the participants.*

Variation 3 – Leading text with space – Solo: Working solo again with your own text, move to a different space in the room for each new thought or variation in your chosen text, even a subtle one – so each change in the space corresponds to a change in the text. Small changes might result in a modest change in space: maybe a level or a turn. Bigger changes might require more radical choices: finding a new place far away, exaggerated shifts in level. Your dynamic in change of space may also reflect dynamics in the text: is it slow or fast? Accelerating or slowing down? You may either choose a new space for each shift or start to identify certain spaces corresponding to different sections in the text. These choices may be useful when moving to *Variation 4*

The full group can do this together while making sure to use peripheral vision and move with full care of others in the room, half of the group can watch the other half, or the group can watch each other one at a time.

Variation 4: Assign a variety of characters to your text, each character assigned to one of the places you have chosen – irrespective of the meaning of the monologue!

Examples might be to perform sections of monologue as:

A commentator
A romantic
A tragedian
A rapper
A politician
As if singing lullaby …

Note: If you are working with a workshop leader they might allow the solos to unfold in the following way, otherwise work on this for yourself in solo practice:

First run through: no particular indication of character, as participant goes through their monologue.

Second run through: the workshop leader proposes three or four characters. If this is done quietly, only intended for participant, observers can guess afterwards which characters were performed.

You are again putting your memorised text into a new context – think of it almost like a musical improvisation – our aim is not to fix things, but to find a new way in – to loosen your intellectual hold on the material to allow an instinctive relationship to it.

Watch each workshop participant in turn and offer feedback to each other – offer character suggestions that might help the speaker expand on their choices, if they have a tendency towards a type, suggest the opposite to help them recognize and then combat this tendency. Try to work with archetypes (e.g. a mother) rather than stereotypes (e.g. a mother-in-law).

Variation 5 – Surprise yourself …: Play with the text to discover new possibilities or shake loose habitual delivery: speak the text as fast as you can, as slowly as you can, when you are upside down, as if you were under water, as if you were a bubble, et cetera.

The remaining exercises in this chapter offer other pathways to the work of Roy Hart and Roy Hart Theatre by former company members and/or certified Roy Hart teachers who have generously offered extracts of their workshop practice here. We thank Noah Pikes, David Goldsworthy, Pascale Ben and Edda Heeg for their kind collaboration with us in bringing this work to you. These exercises can be used variously in combination with the exercises above.

EXPLORING HEIGHT AND DEPTH: THE LIFT BY NOAH PIKES

The following exercise: *The Vertical Axis – Slippery Slopes or Careful Staircase* can be done alone, in pairs, or in a small group. This is based on an image to guide us: *The* Lift, contributed here by RHT company member Noah Pikes.

> **Noah Pikes** was born in wartime London. He began study with Roy Hart in 1967, performing in inaugural and subsequent Roy Hart Theatre performances. He started teaching in 1973, moving with the group to France in 1975. He also studied movement, contemporary dance, clown and jazz improvisation, and collaborated in a multi-octave 'voice-music' group. In 2000, he moved to Zurich and informally studied Jungian and Post-Jungian psychology, developing the 'Whole Voice' approach. He authored *Dark Voices: The Genesis of Roy Hart Theatre* (2019, first published by Spring Publications in 1999). In London, together with David Carey in 2000, he co-led the London International Conference on The Contribution of Alfred Wolfsohn, Roy Hart and Roy Hart Theatre to Vocal Expression.

Noah's note: *For Wolfsohn and Hart one of the principles guiding the work on the voice was summed up in the phrase 'Height based on depth'. By giving ourselves to this sound journey we confront the twin extremes in our voices and in ourselves: the dizzying heights and the dark cave of the deep. These places can scare us, but they can also be territories of heady freedom and anchored bass. In going beyond the zones of civilised speech or even singing in a strict sense, you access the enveloping tissue of sound that surrounds us from infancy to old age: a huge palette of resonance can be charged within our emotional imagination. The Lift permits us to call up this rainbow of sound and lets us experience it directly in a dynamic journey through our bodies.*

4.14 THE LIFT BY NOAH PIKES

Ascent and descent

We've all had the experience of being in a lift, the moment of starting and stopping. Getting in, getting out ... the sensation of rising and falling.

Close your eyes a moment: imagine a lift starting at your feet and working its way up to the top of your head. Once it arrives take a big in-breath as you step into the lift and close the gate. Then visualise it starting its descent.

Let your breath follow that slippery slope down, so it comes out slowly till you get down to the very bottom.

Do this several times, until you have begun to feel the sensation of your breath dropping down as the lift descends. Then try starting at the bottom of the lift. Breath in, and as you enter the lift, start breathing out as you try to catch the sensation of the breath rising in your body until you reach the top of the lift and step out. The lift shaft is inside of you. It is you!

Once you have explored this direction several times, alternate breathing out as you descend, and breathing out as you ascend. Allow several breath cycles once you have arrived at your destination before the in-breath and another lift journey either up or down. Find a rhythm in this.

Gradually introduce vocal sound into the breath, starting again at the top of the lift. At the beginning, you might like to use a soft yawn-like sigh as you step into the lift, dropping down to a breathy warm purr as you stop out at the bottom and exit.

Now increase the vocal sound whilst reducing any breathiness, until you start with increasingly high notes as you enter the lift, dropping to your lowest as you land at the bottom. Similarly, on returning, try entering the lift on your lowest sound and let the sound swoop upwards as the lift travels to the top of your head. You can try this also with different open vowel sounds, becoming aware of any changes in your pitch or perception of your vertical journeys up or down. Try the journey faster or slower.

Side coaching*: Does the speed affect the sound and your feeling / perception? How does your body react to different speeds and the varied open sounds? Try and let your whole body and concentration follow the ascent or descent. Does your body feel different inside? Do your arms change position as you move up and* *down? How does gravity manifest itself in your body and voice? What different feelings are evoked in resisting or giving in to gravity?*

If you have explored so far and feel comfortable, see if you can go a step further.

The slippery slope

Give yourself some 'locations' for where the lift stops: you might experience walking out on to the roof of a skyscraper or a jagged mountain, or you may descend to a dark cave or basement. Let your imagination and voice be influenced by these locations. How does it feel to be on top of the mountain? Do you want to scream for joy? How is it at the bottom of the cave? Do you want to roar aggressively or groan in horror? Explore the different emotions that accompany your journeys.

The careful staircase

Now, you may want to get out at one of the intermediate stops the lift can make instead of going all the way to the top or bottom in one long journey. What happens if you get out on the way and hold for a moment the sound you have at that point? Where do you arrive? Are you on a flat plain with distant horizons or have you arrived in a high gothic church that is filled with your sound? Experiment with different stopping-off points, either going down or up. Does it change depending on whether you are ascending or descending? Are there some surprising sounds, unexpected or even slightly uncontrolled? At this point in *The Lift* experience feel free to breathe in during the journeys and use more out-breaths to cover the full arc of your journey. This way you can spend more time climbing or falling, more time alighting at an intermediate state, or more time once you arrive at your final destination, so you really can 'taste' these places and all they bring in terms of your perception of your own sound, body and feelings.

Noah's note: *Just producing these sounds can be a thrill or a frightening shock.*

The journey can take many forms and shapes. It can lead you to an ecstatic height or a booming depth. It might shoot out in a piercing scream or descend to a low grunt. Explore these contrasts. Let your voice travel through all the lift stops not just the exits at the top and bottom.

If you do this journey alone, allow yourself about 20 minutes including the stages of visualisation, using the breath to travel up and down, gradually breaking into sound, and finally experimenting with some variations. Then give yourself 10 minutes to write down what has happened for you, noting any feelings/sensations that came spontaneously and what you noticed about your voice.

If you can, do The Lift with a partner: that way you can alternate and be stimulated by your partner's journeys and sounds, while remaining true to your own pathways. At the end, you can even practise doing it together, entering and exiting the lift together. Breath as often as you need! Afterwards exchange verbally about your experience and give each other some 'feedback' on what you have noticed about your partner's voice, what surprised you and what you discovered about doing it together.

PASSING THE SOUND BY DAVID GOLDSWORTHY

> **David Goldsworthy** is a founder member of Roy Hart Theatre since 1969, performing in many of the company's shows from 1970 onwards, including *and*, *Three Moods*, *Enchanté*, *Moby Dick* and *Enthousiasme* that he co-directed with Joseph Clark. Since 1990 David has continued to create and collaborate on performances both independently and through his association Diapason, working with a wide range of musicians and artists on over a dozen original works. Recently he teamed up with four other founder members of Roy Hart Theatre to create *Generation* under the musical guidance of Sašo Vollmeier, with performances in France, Italy and Switzerland, co-produced by the Roy Hart International Artistic Centre. David has an established reputation as a teacher in France, and is recognised as a reference in many European countries, including the UK, Ireland, Belgium, Sweden and Switzerland, and has taught at the Vastavox conference.

David's note: *This is primarily a group experience and encourages the group to listen empathetically to each other, thus creating a cohesive quality that can lead into a period of dynamic improvisation. It can be prefaced by a short session that brings awareness of how vowel and vocal quality are linked, awakening the play of the whole vocal apparatus and face. Our voices begin to connect with imagination and emotion.*

4.15 PASSING THE SOUND BY DAVID GOLDSWORTHY

To begin

Start with a hum on an MMMMMM: as you hum think you are making an EE sound (as in reed or feed).

Then allow mouth to open slightly still with the EEE sound.

Now gradually open the mouth further: as you do so notice how the vowel sound naturally changes.

When you reach a fully open mouth, releasing the tongue from its position on the EEE you may be closer to an AAA (as in far or father) and then a very open AH (as in fat).

Explore all the sounds you can draw from your mouth between these two extremes without adding a rounding of your lips.

David's note: *Feel how even small changes in position of tongue and openness of mouth influence the sound. Let your face follow the changes in your tongue and mouth, and feel how these changes affect your feelings and sense of yourself. Watch the changes in others too. As you continue to sing through these changes, make it a kind of love song, not a cold exercise. Making any kind of sound is an imaginative and emotional process.*

Experiment

Now, try experimenting with rounding your lips, once again starting from a relatively closed mouth perhaps on an EE (as in ear) with slightly rounded lips, travelling to an open mouth, widely rounded protruding lips on an OW (as in cow).

David's note: *Once again let this become a love song, a celebration of the diversity of voices you can draw from yourself playing with the degree of roundedness of your lips and the openness of your mouth.*

Finally combine these two experiences so you sing a rich song, poly-vowelled and nuanced. Notice how you enjoy the sensuality of the sound in the way mouth, tongue and lip find innumerable combinations and subtle sound changes. Notice how your soft palette becomes involved and plays along with the other three parts of your vocal apparatus. And let all this spread into your whole face and being so you are fully alive and breathing with this dynamic love song. Watch the others too ...

Group in a circle

A 'throws' a spontaneous – strong – sound, a cry, to B

B 'catches' the sound with another spontaneous sound and then 'throws' a strong sound, a cry, rapidly to C with a second, different sound. This continues around the circle, so all experience both 'catching' and 'throwing' sound. You can mime these gestures too.

David's note: *I often begin a session in a circle throwing sound to each other as an energetic beginning. The sounds are sent dynamically with breath force and should not be hoarse, broken or blocked in the throat. We begin with one sound, then add a second and maybe a third, as if three or four balls of sound are being thrown in the circle, needing a lot of presence and reactivity from everyone.*

4.16: PASSING THE SOUND/IMAGE

Based on passing the sound/image among the group. Image in this sense being understood as a physicalisation of the vocal quality – a form of characterisation that can be mimed by another participant.

Everyone stands in a circle.

1st turn around the circle

Participant A creates a sound/image and passes it on to participant B who imitates it perfectly (as closely as possible!) then transforms it *fluidly* into another very contrasted sound/image without a break or rupture (no sudden jumps) and then passes on to participant C and on around the circle.

David's note: *The first aim of this is to explore the extended range of the voice to express unusual and imaginative sounds, and to create spontaneous characters, animals etc. The student is asked to consciously explore a wide range of sound qualities, going from head sounds (EEE) to chest sounds (AAH) and pelvis sounds (OH and OOO), helped by facial movements and descriptive gestures, and to move the sounds from depth to height looking for the organic connections between sound qualities.*

Ideally, the student should only pass on the sound when something concrete has been 'given birth' to.

The second person is then obliged to tune in to the expressive vocal landscape of the predecessor, to adopt their sounds and attitudes, then to transform these PROGRESSIVELY into a totally different image. There is a lot to be gained by 'living' rather than by 'doing'.

2nd turn around the circle

Participants A and B (face-to-face) co-ordinate to create together another sound/image then pass it on to the next couple (C and D) who then transform it carefully together and pass it on to E and F et cetera.

David's note: *Same as 1st turn but with the added 'problem' of adapting constantly to one's partner, trying to compose together, rather than just 'free expression'.*

3rd turn around the circle

Similar to 2nd turn but now involving three people who strive to create a sound/image/movement together and pass on to the next group of three.

For each subsequent turn of the circle, one person more is added, until the whole group is involved and working towards creating a collective sound/image. Depending on the level of comfort and experience in the work, the group can then, possibly, take this exercise towards an improvisation with more personal freedom.

As a finality to the group exercise, once they are all embroiled together with a common expression, they are suggested to bring more personal ideas, improvise more freely, but remaining connected, and sensitive to the ensemble, then coming together again to finish. A possible culmination of this exercise/impro could be to converge towards a song, or text they've already learnt.

THREE LETTERS, THREE TIMES, THREE MINUTES BY PASCALE BEN

> **Pascale Ben** met Roy Hart and the collected group in 1969 in London, and became a founder member of the company, contributing to its installation at Malérargues and performing in many of its original pieces until its disbanding in 1990. Pascale often composes the music for her songs, although musicians like Christophe Back and Olivier Phillipson have also written specially for her voice. She has an acute sensibility to the alchemy of voice and text, collaborating with a constellation of musicians, directors and performers, creating over 20 highly personal and characterful performances, recitals and concerts.

4.17 THREE LETTERS, THREE TIMES, THREE MINUTES BY PASCALE BEN

P T A

With your lips make P P P P P just with air as long as it goes, six or seven times. And now slower, letting your cheeks blow air with very supple lips. Then one P only, exploding a little and breathing in every time.

Do it again.

Naturally at some point voice will join in this emission of the P as if you are speaking, and you let the sound go up and down a bit, breathing when you wish, and describe curves with P, your cheeks and voice swelling with air.

Do it between ten and twenty times.

Now leave P and visit T.

You make a T, then a series of Ts, TTTTTT, your tongue touching your teeth. You repeat this several times. Then you slow it down, almost stuttering and let the sound of your voice come through, as if you are giving yourself courage. Let the pauses be natural and taste the moments of silence which are not empty but full of what has been and is to come. You are now making TATATA. Now your voice can travel by itself, turning, falling, jumping, spiralling up and down. Sometimes you repeat something that has been particularly enjoyable and each time your voice gets stronger. Very peacefully like a little car riding on a hilly landscape, enjoy the country and the hills and the forests, the villages, the gardens and orchards.

And now PTA

Say PTA PTA PTA PTA PTA PTA PTA, then breathe and repeat PTA PTA PTA PTA PTA PTA PTA and breathe again. Repeat this several times. Now you can make the sound a little higher and next time a little deeper, again and again. Listen to what comes out of you. It is now a little melody. Don't change the height of the sound too often, enjoy repeating what you like several times. It's like Winnie the Pooh humming, it feels quite natural and pleasant.

Voila!

It was Three Minutes with Three Letters, Three Times a day, a very good medicine indeed!

For fun, enjoy making PTAAAAA...... PTAAAA........ Are you yawning?

Bravo! BRAVO!

You have successfully achieved the first set of three, three, three.

M N A

Think of something nice to eat and make very gentle sounds MMMMMMM, as long as you can, several times. This MMMMMMM is a little dog you take for a walk in a beautiful landscape.

Your mouth is closed, and you gently let your chin come down, as you make the MMMMMMM sound of pleasure. Gradually you are making a space in your mouth like a high grotto. Do this several times. You will notice that the sound amplifies and grows, and it also resonates in your head. Enjoy it!

Then, the letter N, several times, and breathe and do it again, thinking of all things you don't like and which bother you: NNNNNN as your tongue pushes against your upper teeth and gum ridge. Listen to the sound and take pleasure at this vibration in your head.

Now let it go up and down smoothly with the same volume all the time, an average volume, breathing when you need to, is it pleasant? Do it again.

And add the A: NNNNNA NNNNNAAAAAAA, and bring back the M: MNAAAAAAA, MNAAAAAA, and now let your sound swell, listening to your voice. Does it want to stay there, or to go deeper, to go up? Follow it like a kite in the wind ...

O U I

A comedy ghost in the night with a white frock and chains, it feels very lonely and moans OU! OU! Like the owl in the forest, howling sounds like the hungry wolf: OU! OU! From deep to high, looking at the lake and singing to the moon. HOU HOU HOU!

And now the sound O like when you say the floor, the door, poor me! like the character of Eeyore in *Winnie-the-Pooh*. Think of how miserable life sometimes is, and moan, moan, and howl, and moan – Poor Me! Poor Me! – and the colour of your voice goes down, becomes darker and deeper. Practise this a little.

Then the wind comes and pushes the clouds away: OU-I (pronounce EEEEE). This sound encourages you to smile. Here comes the sun! O U I O U I O U I!

You are in a Montgolfier (hot-air])balloon, in the sky and now prepare yourself to land again. Safely slowly land and come back to silence, enjoy this silence. It is full. It gives value to the sounds you have made; they live in your memory. And, yes, listen to the sounds that exist around you.

Make this journey as often as you please!

Finally, repeat the word Y E S staying on the beginning of the word a longer time than usual, then sounding the SSSS too.

And a quote from A.A. Milne's *The House at Pooh Corner*: *'For a long time they looked at the river beneath them, saying nothing, and the river said nothing too, for it felt very quiet and peaceful on this summer afternoon'* (Milne 1928: 108).

My advice to someone wanting to discover their voice: move, move and MOVE so that you can BE MOVED in return.

Pull FACES, making one face, and then another, avoid squinting, or anything damaging.

Now go from one face to another very slowly, and that's called in French *'FONDU-ENCHAINE'* Then your voice joins in and makes sounds that go with the movements of your face. AND EVEN SLOWER. And also louder. It relaxes tensions at a very deep level.

Blowing a raspberry

Dorothy, Roy's wife and Jonathan's mother, was my singing teacher to start with, and she told me that from her point of view, I was taking myself far too seriously. Then she gave me homework, that was to *blow 20 raspberries* in front of the mirror every morning.

You stand on your two feet, looking at yourself, you breathe in. Then while breathing out, let you tongue come out of your mouth very relaxed. With your lips around your tongue, blow and it sounds rather like a fart, making a vast quantity of *postillons* (spit!)!

It is pleasant to do, but when you are alone only.

Pascale' note: *Most of the exercises I have described to you are to be performed in your single presence, and not heard by other people as they can be 'dérangeants' (disturbing) for other persons who might be listening. Be careful, full of care.*

TOUCH – BE IN TOUCH – BE TOUCHED: THROUGH TOUCH INTO VOICE TOWARDS MUSIC BY EDDA HEEG

> **Edda Heeg** was born in Germany in 1967. She began studying music, singing and the violin at the Hanover Conservatory of Music and Theatre and continued her music studies at the Folkwang Conservatory in Essen, receiving her Diploma in Music Pedagogy in 1994. She started teaching at the CAIRH/Malérargues in 1996. In 1998 she opened The Roy Hart Voice Centre, Hanover/Germany, etage2. Since 2008 she has been teaching at the Acting Department at the Conservatory of Music and Theatre in Hanover. Beside her musical studies, Edda focuses a lot on movement in relation to voice work. Edda has worked as a singer and performing artist for various projects and theatres, as well as in a number of performances at the Roy Hart Centre.

Edda's note: For me the 'magic' always happens when the pupil stops trying, stops 'exercising', and lets go of wanting and of his or her own judgemental expectations. Then it starts to sing, 'The mystery behind the voice appears' (Wolfsohn 2012: 31). The individual work with one person is certainly the core work of our tradition, going back to Alfred Wolfsohn's approach. But it often needs the group frame to make these moments possible. It is the energy which is generated during the warm-up classes and reinforced in the 'atelier-work', which builds up the heat for these 'magic moments'. From my point of view, one of the most important elements in our voice work is 'connection': the ability to connect to the space and energy around you, and thus to your voice and body, and through these connections to yourself. This connection often can be created by TOUCH. In the Wolfsohn/Hart voice work the touch, in partner or group exercises, allows a very intense encounter with the voice and oneself. 'Being touched' means, on one level, the physical quality of warming up the body, but it also has an emotional impact on the person receiving it. To let oneself be touched, to allow someone to 'get under your skin', implies a letting go of our protective armour and rigid expectations, as we surrender to that touch: thus paving the way for revealing fresh layers and strands in our voice. To touch somebody, one needs to be in touch with oneself and at the same time in contact with the partner. One needs to build up a great deal of empathy and 'physical listening', in order to step into *the energy field of somebody else and follow their needs with the right quality of touch: accompanying, supporting, sometimes guiding or manipulating. I offer here a series of exercises/pathways on the topic.*

4.18 TOUCH – BE IN TOUCH – BE TOUCHED: THROUGH TOUCH INTO VOICE TOWARDS MUSIC BY EDDA HEEG

This sequence of exercises is designed for a group of 8–12 people. Each exercise builds on the previous exercises, but can also be incorporated elsewhere in a lesson plan.

Move in space

For this kind of work you should start with a physical warm-up: walking, bouncing, running, opening the energetic field in the space, looking out while moving, being aware of the group. You can use rhythmical music to establish this kind of connection with the space.

Holding the earth globe – MOA-circle

Come to a circle.

Breath out with open mouth. While exhaling you open your arms as if you are holding a big ball in your arms, like holding the earth globe: slightly bent knees with the breathing out.

While breathing in, let your arms sink down and experience how to allow the air to come in passively through open mouth. Make sure there is no breathing sound. The 'channel of the breath' is wide open. As you inhale you come back up again, slightly stretching the legs.

After some time you add a sound on the syllable (MOA) on one note, when you breath out. Open up the sound into the circle of your arms and further into the circle of the group, each out-breath on a new pitch. While singing, listen to the harmonies and clusters developing in the group. Choose consciously your next pitch according to the music you hear around you.

Look around into the circle. Connect yourself with the group.

While doing this several times, feel your presence opening up more and more.

Feel the global energy of the group increasing.

Let go.

Standing. Find a bouncing up and down motion initiated from ankle and knee. Let the voice move freely with each dropping down. Passive inhaling while bouncing up, mouth stays open.

MOA-circle into sound cloud

You start again the *MOA-tones* with lifting the arms (*Holding the earth globe*) three times.

After that, with each *MOA-tone*, you take one or two steps forward to cross the circle. You will adapt the movements of your arms while passing and touching others who are also crossing the circle. You are weaving a sound carpet, first coming close together and then continuing your path on the other side of the circle. By moving on into the room *the sound cloud* is opening up, the sounds are connecting more and more in space. Sometimes you stop and stand close to each other, let two or three voices sing together, then walk on and find new constellations.

The *sound cloud* can also be experienced with the eyes closed, if the group is already confident enough.

Let go.

You stay somewhere in the space and start again the bouncing motion, shake yourself to relax body and voice.

4.19 FOUR TOUCHES (COUPLE WORK)

Find a partner. One person is receiving touch and transforming it into sound. This person can move (staying on the spot, going to the floor, or moving into space).

The partner is touching this person with different touch qualities (~5 minutes each) in the following order:

(a) massaging
(b) stroking
(c) pushing/pulling/manipulating
(d) wafer-thin touch

Change roles.

Edda's note: *The voice liberates itself by developing various voice qualities, not by producing sound consciously, but by letting go. The 'sounder' shouldn't* *control their voice, but follow the body impulses. Unreflected sounds – yawning, sighing, grunting, laughter – are very important in preparing the voice to free itself from censuring self- judgment.*

Back-to-back leading ear-to-ear

Two people are leaning with their backs towards each other, bent legs.

They move back-to-back while sounding freely. Sound into the back of your partner. Connect with the voice of the partner. Sometimes the movement can be very soft, sometimes one can give more energy, pushing the partner backwards. The duo should seek the right balance of weight and energy so legs and spine don't tire.

Working with the lower back is always helpful for the voice. It activates the posterior diaphragm lobes. It increases the connection into the legs and the lower energy centres.

While gently pushing into the back of your partner, you sink down together into the floor, first to a sitting position then to lying down with your heads lying on the shoulder of your partner, ear-to-ear: your bodies are stretched out on the floor in opposite directions. Breathe together. One starts to sing softly, the partner answers, leading into an improvised musical duet.

You roll apart, find a space for yourself without physical contact. Be silent and aware of your breathing and the connection to yourself. Listen to the echo of your voice journey.

4.20 AMOEBA (GROUP EXPLORATION)

Lying on the back alone, with eyes closed

Imagine yourself like an amoeba, a one-cell organism which is moving through an ocean of breath and sound.

> Start rolling /moving on the floor in slow motion.
> While moving let the voice sound on each out-breath.
> Move slowly into space and connect with other voices.
> Seek for physical contact, but feel free to find your own space.
> Search for musical encounters.

This phase should be long. It should give enough time to dive into the universe of listening, moving into close contact, sounding together, with eyes closed.

This exercise represents the development from one cell into one big organism created by all the participants. In this exploration every sound is welcome and the participants can use the various possibilities of their voice, not only what is usually called 'singing'.

Pausing: be aware of any kind of emotions coming up; feel your breath, the connection to the other bodies surrounding or touching you.

Solo with support

The group is continuing to move without sounding. Eventually open the eyes.

One or two persons at a time (depending on the size of the group) receive the focus and physical support of the group as they continue the vocal journey.

Everybody experiences this solo or duo moment.

Edda's note: *The supporting group should be very aware of HOW they touch and accompany the soloist(s) so they support them in their vocal journey, and enable them to use the wealth of information the touch imparts to step outside their habitual patterns. It is an exploration of the vocal possibilities within the 'emotional landscapes' of one's voice. The soloist can also be asked to use a song or text they are familiar with so they can explore it afresh in this context.*

Musical improvisation with piano

The whole group comes back to sounding and moving, with or without physical contact, but still in the spirit of the 'amoeba-ocean'.

The participants leave pauses to hear each other.

The piano joins in with one low note. Then more and more harmonics are added, bringing the group into a common musical improvisation.

By giving a common musical frame, the capacity of listening to each other can be increased and the group can experience a common space of sound and music.

BIBLIOGRAPHY

Many performance scripts and annotated scripts, media coverage, company correspondence and recordings were accessed at the RHT Archive at Malérargues.

Centre Artistique International Roy Hart (CAIRH) is the official organisation, currently based at the company's site at Malérargues, France, which hosts workshops and productions and training (https://roy-hart-theatre.com/).

Company member and archivist Paul Silber has also compiled much material on http://www.roy-hart.com/ (this website's URL is very similar to that of CAIRH above – note that these are two different resources).

Images used here in Chapters 1–3 can be found at the Roy Hart Theatre Photographic Archives, by Ivan Midderigh, at https://www.royharttheatrephotographicarchives.com/.

Abulafia, John (1969) review, *Time Out*, December.

Adlington, Robert (ed.) (2020) *New Music Theatre in Europe: Transformations between 1955–1975*. London & New York: Routledge.

Almuro, Andre (1972) *Visit to Godenhall*, recorded in December for ORTF (French National Radio).

Anderson, Kaya (1969) annotated text of *The Bacchae*. RHT Archive.

Anderson, Kaya (2015) 'The Transmission of Alfred Wolshohn's Legacy to Roy Hart'. Available at https://roy-hart-theatre.com/shop/the-transmission-of-alfred-wolfsohns-legacy-to-roy-hart/

Anderson, Kaya (2018) interview with Kevin Crawford, 1 July.

Armstrong, Richard (2018) interview with Kevin Crawford, 18 & 21 January.

Artaud, Antonin (1938) *Le Théâtre et son Double*, Paris: Gallimard.

Artaud, Antonin (1958) *The Theatre of Cruelty*, in *The Theatre and its Double* translated by Mary Caroline Richards. New York: Grove Press.

Artaud, Antonin (1964) *Les Cenci*, in *Œuvres completes*. Paris: Gallimard.

Artaud, Antonin (1969) *The Cenci*, London: Calder and Boyars.

Artaud, Antonin (1958) *The Theatre and its Double*, translated by Mary Caroline Richards. New York: Grove Press.

Backès-Clément, C. (1972) review, *Lettres Françaises*, 23 May.

Barnes, Mary and Joseph Berk (1971) *Two Accounts of a Journey Through Madness*. California & New York: Harcourt Brace Jovanovich.

Béhar, Serge (1972) *Biodrame*. RHT Archive. Also available at http://www.roy-hart.com/bio1.htm

Béhar, Serge and Roy Hart Theatre (1975) *L'Economiste*. RHT Archive.

Berberian, Cathy (1966) 'The New Vocality in Contemporary Music'. Available at https://www.taylorfrancis.com/books/edit/10.4324/9781315571072/cathy-berberian-pioneer-contemporary-vocality-pamela-karantonis-francesca-placanica-pieter-verstraete?refId=afc64bc4-7b0c-4df3-86be-05001651f2f5&context=ubx

Beschreibung der Inneren Erfahrungen (*Descriptions of an Inner Experience*) (1972) Meinhard Rudenauer, Austrian Radio, 17 January, Internationale Gesellschaft für Neue Musik (International Society for New Music). Referenced in RHT Archive.

Billington, Michael (1969) 'New View of *The Bacchae*', *The Times*, 27 October.

Biodrame (1973) review from unspecified Barcelona newspaper; reviewer unknown. Referenced in RHT Archive.

Borrelly, M. (1969), review, *L'Est Républicain*, 24 April.

Braggins, Sheila (2011) *The Mystery Behind the Voice*. Leicester: Matador.

Brook, Peter (1966) personal letter to Roy Hart and Roy Hart Theatre. RHT Archive.

Buber, Martin (2008) *I and Thou*, translated by Walter Kaufman. New York: Simon & Schuster. First published in 1923.

Cadieu, Martine (1969) review, in *Lettres Françaises*, August, translated by Kevin Crawford.

Crawford, Kevin (2019) interview with Bernadette Sweeney, 15 August.

Crawford, Kevin and Noah Pikes (2019) 'Vocal Traditions: The Roy Hart Tradition', *Voice and Speech Review* 19(2): 237–48. Available at https://doi.org/10.1080/23268263.2019.1576998 or available at https://kevincrawfordvoice.com/articles/

Curtin, Adrian (2009) 'Alternative Vocalities: Listening Awry to Peter Maxwell Davies's "Eight Songs for a Mad King"', *Mosaic: An Interdisciplinary Critical Journal* 42(2): 101–17.

Darmstadter Echo (1969) review of *Spirale*, 9 April.

de Jongh, Nicholas (1969) review, *The Guardian*, 16 December.

Dorothy and Her Fellow Women Soloists (2007) CD. RHT Archive.

Dort, Bernard (1969) 'Illusion and Action', *Politique Aujourd'hui*, June–July.

Engweth, Ruediger (1972) review, *Salzburger Nachrichten*, 20 January.

Frenkel, Louis (1972) private letter. RHT Archive.

Gauthier, Jean-Jacques (1972) review, *Le Figaro*, 19 April.

George, Nadine (2020) interview with Kevin Crawford, 10 January.

The Guardian (2016) 'Obituary: Sir Peter Maxwell Davies' 16 March. Available at https://www.bbc.com/news/entertainment-arts-20683877

Hart, Dorothy (1969) 'Dot's Visualisation of a stage in their growth of *The Bacchae* into *The Frontae* into *The Holy Ghost*'. RHT Archive.

Hart, Dorothy (1969) 'God is dead. Long live …?' programme note for *The Bacchae*. RHT Archive. Available at http://www.roy-hart.com/Bacchae1968.htm

Hart, Dorothy (1969) notes on the production *The Bacchae-The Frontae*. RHT Archive. Available at http://www.roy-hart.com/frontae.htm

Hart, Dorothy (1972) a rehearsal note for *and*. RHT Archive. Available at http://www.roy-hart.com/dorothy.htm

Hart Dorothy (1975) *L'Economist: A Dream of Reality*, March. RHT Archive.

Hart, Jonathan (n.d) *The Wild is Rising*, CD. RHT Archive. Available at https://open.spotify.com/album/6tTYN1eAaQTCoibPhF4GbM

Hart, Jonathan (2020) interview with Kevin Crawford, 10 January.

Hart, Roy (n.d) 'And Man had a Voice'. Available at https://music.apple.com/us/album/and-man-had-a-voice/1219991775?ign-mpt=uo%3D4

Hart, Roy (n.d) *The Rock* by T.S. Eliot. Available at https://www.youtube.com/watch?v=oqBtZL9pP28

Hart, Roy (1947) unpublished diary. RHT Archive.

Hart, Roy (1966) personal letter to the Roy Hart Company. RHT Archive.

Hart, Roy (1967) *How a Voice Gave me a Conscience*. Available at http://www.roy-hart.com/hvgmc.htm

Hart, Roy (1969) interview with Peter Haley-Dunne. RHT Archive.

Hart, Roy (1970) personal letter to the Roy Hart Company. RHT Archive.

Hart, Roy (1971) letter to James Roose-Evans. RHT Archive.

Hart, Roy (1972) 'The Objective Voice'. Available at www.roy-hart.com/objective.voice.htm

Hart, Roy (1972) programme note for concert by ORTF (French National Radio), France, June. RHT Archive.

Hart, Roy (1973) annotated text of *Biodrame*. RHT Archive.

Hart, Roy (1973) '*Biodrame*….is somewhat the story of my life'. RHT Archive. Available at http://www.roy-hart.com/pauls.htm

Hart, Roy (1973) letter on *Biodrame*. RHT Archive.

Hart, Roy (1973) private letter to Roy Hart Theatre. RHT Archive.

Hart, Roy (1974) letter to Serge Béhar. RHT Archive.

Harvey, Robert (1975) *L'Economiste* programme note. RHT Archive.

Henze, Hans Werner (1968) *Versuch über Schweine* (*Essay on Pigs*). Available at https://www.youtube.com/watch?v=AE6Xn1dsgqo

Henze, Hans Werner (1998) *Bohemian Fifths*. London: Faber and Faber.

Hewett, Ivan (2007) 'Karlheinz Stockhausen', *The Guardian*, 7 December. Available at https://www.theguardian.com/music/2007/dec/07/7

Hillman, James (1979) *Dream and the Underworld*. New York: Harper and Row.

Institut del Teatre (1973) review of *Biodrame*, February. RHT Archive.

Johnson, Robert A. (1986) *Inner Work: Using Dreams and Active Imagination for Personal Growth*. New York: Harper and Row.

Jones, Nicholas (ed.) (2020) *Peter Maxwell Davies, Selected Writings*. Cambridge: Cambridge University Press.

Jung, C.G (1955) *Modern Man in Search of a Soul*. New York: Harcourt Brace. First published in 1933.

Jung, C.G. (1968) *Man and his Symbols*. New York: Dell Publishing Co. Inc. First published in 1964.

Kretzmer, Herbert (1969) review, *The Daily Express*, 16 December.

Krüger, Anne-Marie (2014) 'Fokus Darmstadt. Case studies of performance practice'. Dieser Aufsatz entstand im Rahmen des SNF-Forschungsprojektes Fallbeispiele der Aufführungspraxis der Neuen Musik 1946–1990 an der Hochschule für Musik Basel, FSP I/B Abbildung 1: 25–7

La Peste (*The Plague*) (1972) by Antonin Artaud with jazz pianist George Grüntz, for West Deutsche Rundfunk in Cologne, directed by Paul Pörtner.

Laing, R.D. and A. Esterson (1970) *Sanity, Madness, and the Family: Families of Schizophrenics*. Baltimore, MD: Penguin.

Le Monde (1975) 'The Morality of Roy Hart Theatre', 22 August.

Le Petit Cevenol (1975) review of *L'Economiste*. RHT Archive.

Magilton, Ian (2019) interview with Kevin Crawford, December.

Mann, William (1969) 'A garland for Dr. Kalmus', *The Times*, 23 April.

Marcus, Frank (1968) 'An Orgy of Therapy', *Sunday Telegraph* 1 December.

Maxwell Davies, Peter (2014) *Eight Songs for a Mad King*. BBC Sounds.

Maxwell Davies, Peter (1968) letter to Hart. RHT Archive.

Maxwell Davies, Peter (2014) interview at Cheltenham music festival, 17 May. Available at https://www.bbc.co.uk/sounds/play/p01z9jcc

McClary, Susan (2020) 'Cathy Berberian – Modernism's Bette Midler'. Foreword to Adlington, Robert (ed.) *New Music Theatre in Europe: Transformations between 1955–1975*. London & New York: Routledge.

Milne, A.A. (1928) *The House at Pooh Corner*. New York: American Book-Stratford Press Inc. Reprint 1961.

Monleón, José (1976) review, *Triunfo*, 14 February.

Monleón, José, Pepe Estruch and Ricardo Domenech (1971) *Primer Acto*. RHT Archive.

Moore, Boris (1975) programme notes for *L'Economiste and the Music*. RHT Archive.

Nayeri, Farah (2018)'109 Players. 3 Conductors. It's even harder than it sounds.' *New York Times*, 29 June. Available at https://www.nytimes.com/2018/06/29/arts/music/gruppen-stockhausen-tate-modern.html

The Nobel Prize (n.d.) *All Nobel Prizes in Literature*. Available at https://www.nobelprize.org/prizes/lists/all-nobel-prizes-in-literature/

Pardo, Enrique (2003) 'Figuring Out the Voice: Object, Subject, Project. Performing Strategies in the Use of Extended Voice Range Techniques in Relation to Language and Texts', *Performance Research* 8(1): 41–50. Available at https://www.pantheatre.com/pdf/6-reading-list-voice-JPR-gb.pdf

Pardo, Enrique (2019) interview with Bernadette Sweeney, 5 July.

Pikes, Noah (2019) *Dark Voices: The Genesis of Roy Hart Theatre*. Zurich: Whole Voice Publishing. First published in 1999.

Pikes, Noah (2020) interview with Kevin Crawford, February.

Placanica, Francesca (2019) 'Embodied Commitments: Solo Performance and the Making of New Music Theatre'. In Adlington, Robert (ed.) *New Music Theatre in Europe: Transformations between 1955–1975*. London & New York: Routledge.

Porter, Andrew (1969) review, *Financial Times*, 15 February.

RADA (1947) Report on Roy Hart. RHT Archive.

RADA (1949) Report on Roy Hart. RHT Archive.

Rickards, Guy (2012) 'Hans Werner Henze Obituary', *The Guardian*, 27 October. Available at: https://www.theguardian.com/music/2012/oct/27/hans-werner-henze

Roose-Evans, James (1996) *Experimental Theatre from Stanislavski to Peter Brook*. London: Routledge.

Roy Hart Explores Rudyard Kipling's 'If' (2003) compiled by Paul Silber, recorded 1963, CD. RHT Archive.

Roy Hart Theatre (n.d) *PreVerbal*, CD. RHT Archive.

Roy Hart Theatre (1968) *The Eight Octave Voice*, facsimile of the 1968 disc. RHT Archive.

Roy Hart Theatre and Leslie Shephard (1964) *The Theatre of Being*, film. RHT Archive.

Sadie, Stanley (1969) review, *The Times*, 15 February.

Salvatore, Gastón (n.d.) *Versuch über Schweine (Essay on Pigs)*, extract translated by Kevin Crawford. RHT Archive.

Serrano, Miguel (1966) *C.G. Jung and Herman Hesse – A Record of Two Friendships*. London: Routledge and Keagan Paul Ltd.

Shaw, Desmond Taylor (1969) review, *Sunday Times*, 27 April.

Silber, Clara (1997) private letter to Noah Pikes. RHT Archive.

Silber, Paul (n.d.) 'The Eight Octave Voice'. Available at http://www.roy-hart.com/8_octive_voice1.htm

Silber, Paul (n.d.) 'Who was Dorothy Hart?' Available at http://www.roy-hart.com/dorothy.htm

Silber, Paul (2018) interview with Kevin Crawford, 6 July.

Silber, Paul (2020) personal essay. RHT Archive.

Silber, Paul and Clara Silber (2020) 'A Celebration of Life', unpublished, May. RHT Archive.

Stockhausen, Karlheinz (1968) letter to Roy Hart, 18 October. RHT Archive.

Turner, Clifford (2007) *Voice and Speech in the Theatre*. London: Methuen Drama. First published in 1950.

Vellacott, Philip (1954) *The Bacchae*. London: Penguin Classics.

Vocal Range (1956) New York: Smithsonian Folkways Records. Available at https://folkways.si.edu/vox-humana-alfred-wolfsohns-experiments-in-extension-of-human-vocal-range/contemporary-electronic-science-nature-sounds/album/smithsonian

Volkszeitung Klagenfurt (1975) review of *L'Economiste*, 13 May. RHT Archive.

Vox Humana (1956) recorded and published by Folkways Records, CATALOG NUMBER FW06123, FX 6123. Available at https://folkways.si.edu/vox-humana-alfred-wolfsohns-experiments-in-extension-of-human-vocal-range/contemporary-electronic-science-nature-sounds/album/smithsonian

Wise, Linda (2014) 'Dorothy Hart'. Available at https://roy-hart-theatre.com/legacy/

Wise, Linda (2019) interview with Bernadette Sweeney, 5 July.

Wise, Linda (2021) email correspondence with Bernadette Sweeney, June.

Wolfsohn, Alfred (2012) *Orpheus or The Way to a Mask*. Abraxas Publications. Written in 1937. Available at https://www.royharttheatrephotographicarchives.com/books/download-orpheus-pdf/

Young, Vivienne (1975) programme notes for *The Birth of L'Economiste*. RHT Archive.

INDEX

We have chosen not to itemize Roy Hart or the Roy Hart Theatre in this index, as they are ubiquitous throughout the book.

A Celebration of Life 168
A Song of the Mind 88
Abraxas *Abraxas Club* 37, 72, 89, 96, 104–5; *Philosophy* 61, 89
Abraxas Publications 168
Abulafia, John 85, 161
Allen, Anna 12, 29, 85
Almuro, Andre 29, 161
Amadée 40
Amoeba 158, 159
and (theatre production) 88–95, 88, 104
Anderson, Kaya 2, 7–8, 10, 13, 81, 105, 117, 162
Andrews, Hans 80
Archipelago 40
Armstrong, Richard 2, 23, 35, 39, 40, 78, 84–5, 88, 90, 110, 112, 117, 137, 162

Artaud, Antonin 29, 33, 36, 49, 50, 79, 162, 165
Aus Den Sieben Tagen 27, 28

Bacchae, The 3, 22, 26–7, 31–4, 44, 52, 59, 61–4, 68, 75–87, 76, 92, 104, 162–4, 168
Backès-Clément, C. 94, 162
Barrault, Jean-Louis 1, 93–6
Bausch, Pina 82
Béhar, Serge 35, 38, 53, 66, 69–70
Ben, Pascale 2, 104, 145; *Three Letters, Three Times, Three Minutes* 151–4
Berkoff, Steven 33
Beschreibung[en] der Inneren Erfahrungen (Descriptions of an Inner Experience) 29, 49, 162
Billington, Michael 84, 162

Biodrame 3, 7, 53–55, 93–103, 162, 164–5
Birthday 88
Boettger, Karlheinz 29
Borrelly, M. 82, 163
Braggins, Sheila 10–11, 163
Breath, Bone, Muscle, Sound 120–9
Brook, Peter 1, 14–16, 68, 79, 84, 93, 163, 167

Café de Flora 103–6
Campbell, Patrick 2
Centres of Resonance 139, *140*
Crawford, Kevin 2–3, *3*, 25, 37; *on Roy Hart 41–2*; *The Bacchae* 77, 80, 86; *and* 91; *L'Economiste* 110; *Paradoxes and Pathways* 117; *Kevin's note* 118–122, 133, 142–3; *Violin, Viola, Cello* 134–138, 162–7
Crawford, Monty 12, 16; *Abraxas Club* 31; 37
CUIFERD, the Centre for Theatre Research 35
Curtin, Adrian *Eight Songs for a Mad King* 24–6, 163

Dark Voices 2, 145, 166
Darmstadt 27–8, 165
Darmstadter Echo 28, 163
Deschamps, Lucienne 37, 39, 66, 104, 112
Dia Pasón 148
Dort, Bernard 83, 163

Eights Songs for a Mad King 19, 22–4, 33–4, 48, 52, 60, 84 163, 166
Eliot, T. S. 7–9, 87, 164
Embodied Commitments: Solo Performance and the Making of New Music Theatre' 19, 167

Federico García Lorca's *Lament for the Death of Ignacio Sánchez Mejías* 13, 87
Festival Mondial du Théâtre Universitaire, The 26, 81
Footsbarn 68
Four Touches 157
Frenkel, Louis 12, 16; *Abraxas Club* 31, 77, 163
Furies (1986) 40, 117

George, Nadine 2, 9–14; *Hallelujah Chorus* 91–2, 163
Goldsworthy, David 2, 145; *Passing The Sound* 148–151
Graham, Martha *technique* 32; 89, 120
Grotowski, Jerzy 1, 14–16, 32, 79, 82, 93
Günther, Marita 7–10, 13; *The Bacchae* 77
Grünz, George 36

Hart, Dorothy 10–13, 29, 38–9, 42–44; *Writings* 59–67, 78–86; 76, 93; *L'Economiste* 102–107; 112, 154, 163–68
Hart, Jonathan 2, 10, 108–110, 117, 164
Harvey, Robert 7, 12–13, 29, 32, 36, 41, 62, 66, 77, 80, 88–91, 108–10, 165
Heeg, Edda 2, 145; *Touch – Be in Touch – Be Touched* 155–159
Henze, Hans Werner 18–22, 48, 64–65, 165–7
Hesse, Herman 32, 167
How a Voice Gave me a Conscience 1967 44–48, 164
Huanacu 88

Ibsen, Henrik 4
Ich Bin 36, 102
Instituto de Teatro de Barcelona 36, 101, 162
International Ferienkurse für Neue Musik 27, 29
Irwin, Barrie 12, 18, 32–35, 77, 80, 89, 109–10

Jung, C.G. 7, 32, 116, 145, 165–7

Kaspar (1984) 40
Kidaha, David Makwaia 10
King George III 22–3
Kretzmer, Herbert 87, 165
Kyrie Eleison 29–30

L'Economiste 3, 36–40, 44, 59–60, 66, 102–113, *103*, 162, 165–8
L'Enchanté 40
L'Enthousiasme 40
La Peste (*The Plague*) 29, 165
La Voix Est Libre 40
Laing, R. D. 14, 49, 165
Lalo, Edouard 36
Lang, Jacques 81
Le Monde 112, 165
Le théâtre du cri 89, 94, 105
Les Lumières de l' Été 104–6
Limón, José 89
Lopez Barrantes, Rafael 40, 108

Magilton, Ian 92, 105
Malérargues 37–41, 102–103, 105, 109, 111–112, 117, 138, 151, 155, 161
Mann, Chris 9, 35
Mariage de Lux 35–36, 102–104
Maxwell-Davies, Peter 18–20, 22–26, 48, 64, 84, 163, 165, 166
Mayer, Elizabeth (Liza) 2, 12, 35, 39–40, 43, 77, 112

McClary, Susan 17, 166
Midderigh, Ivan 27, 30, 71, 76, 88, 103, 161
Moby Dick (1989) 40, 148
Monleón, José 4–5, 7, 16, 35, 44, 55–58, 113, 166

Namouna 36
Nexus 29, 88

Owning Our Own Voices, Vocal Discovery in the Wolfsohn-Hart Tradition 2

Pagliacci (1985) 40
Pardo, Enrique 2, 39–40, 57, 72, 95, 110, 166
Passing the Sound 148–150
Pierrot Players, The 23
Pikes, Margaret 2
Pikes, Noah 2, 71, 93, 108, 145–46, 163, 167
Placanica, Francesca 19, 162, 167
Polizzy, Flavio 40
Pörtner, Paul 29, 35, 102, 165
Primer Acto 44, 55, 93, 166

RADA, London 4–7, 42, 46, 98, 167
Redgrove, Peter 9, 34
Riversmore, Gabriel 37
Roagna, Renata 40
Roose-Evans, James 67–8, 164, 167
Rosa, Hebe 33, 89
Rossignol, Derek 4, 7, 13, 16, 32, 80, 89
Roy Hart International Artistic Centre (CAIRH) 41, 155, 161
Rudenauer, Meinhard 29, 49, 162

Sacra-Lumbar Stretch 123–24
Serrano, Miguel 32, 167
Shakespeare, William 15, 40

Silber, Clara 93, 168
Silber, Paul 12, 18, 23, 33, 38–9, 60, 71, 80, 92, 103–4, 110–12, 167
Spiral [Spirale] 19, 27, 84, 163
Stockhausen, Karlheinz 18–19, 27, 168
Stow, Randolph (1935–2010) 22–23, 26
Sweeney, Bernadette 117, 121, 123–24, 127, 163, 166, 168

Teatro El Campesino 82
Tempest (1977) 15, 40, 79, 84, 117
The Abraxas Club 22, 25, 27, 31–34, 72, 89, 96, 104–05
The Bacchae presented as The Frontae 64, 83
The Eight Octave Voice 18, 45, 72
The Lift 145–48
The Living Theatre 85
The Love and Death of Cornet Christopher Rilke 13
The Magic Chord 89–90
The New Vocality in Contemporary Music 17, 162
The Objective Voice 21, 48–51, 164
The Pelvic Clock 120–21, 126–27
The Raft of The Medusa 18, 20
The Singer and The Song 61, 88
The Song of Everest 34
The Theatre of Being (1964) 12, 167

The Times 21, 84, *162*
Theron, Johannes 40
Three Conductors 92
Three Hums: Waking Up Resonance in The Head 129
Three Letters, Three Times, Three Minutes 151–52
Three Moods 36–37, 102, 148
Touch – Be in Touch – Be Touched: Through Touch into Voice Towards Music 155–56
Turner, Clifford 6, 168

Versuch über Schweine (*Essay on Pigs*) (1968) 18, 20–23, 25, 33, 84, 96, 165
Violin, Viola, Cello 133–34, 138
Vladimir Rodzianko 29
Vocal Playfulness 131
Vox Humana 17, 168

Waking Up The Voice 118, 141
Watanka 88
Wilson, Robert 82
Wise, Linda 2, 40, 60–61, 63, 168
Wolfsohn, Alfred 2, 4–8, 10, 16, 20, 41, 44, 46, 53, 55, 72, 92, 98, 134, 145, 155, 168

Young, Vivienne 12, 29, 35, 37–39, 42–43, 58, 66, 102–04, 112, 168

Printed in the United States
by Baker & Taylor Publisher Services